4.95

The Canon of
Reason and Virtue

D1445626

The
Canon of Reason and Virtue

(Lao-tze's Tao Teh King)

Chinese and English

Translated by D. T. Suzuki & Paul Carus

Open  Court
La Salle, Illinois

Publisher's Note
This 1974 Open Court Paperback edition is an un-
abridged reproduction of previous clothbound editions
published in 1964, 1927 and 1913.

Copyright © 1913 and 1927 by
Open Court Publishing Company

Lao-tzu.
    The canon of reason and virtue . . .

    Reprint of the 1964 ed.
    Bibliography: p.
    I. Suzuki, Daisetz Teitaro, 1870-1966, tr. II. Carus, Paul, 1852-
1919, tr. III. Title.
BL1900.L3C35   1974   181'.11   73-21701
ISBN   0-87548-064-0

TABLE OF CONTENTS.

FOREWORD.

This booklet, *The Canon of Reason and Virtue,* is an extract from the author's larger work, *Lao-Tze's Tao Teh King,* and has been published for the purpose of making our reading public more familiar with that grand and imposing figure *Li Er,* who was honored with the posthumous title *Poh-Yang,* i. e., Prince Positive (representing the male or strong principle); but whom his countrymen simply call *Lao-tze,* the Old Philosopher.

* * *

Sze-Ma Ch'ien, the Herodotus of China, who lived about 136-85 B. C., has left a short sketch of Lao-tze's life in his *Shi Ki* (Historical Records) which is here prefixed as the most ancient and only well-attested account to be had of the Old Philosopher.

Born in 604 B. C., Lao-tze was by about half a century the senior of Confucius. He must have attained great fame during his life, for Confucius is reported to have sought an interview with him. But the two greatest sages of China did not understand each other, and they parted mutually disappointed.

Confucius's visit to Lao-tze has been doubted. If it is not historical it certainly is *ben trovato*, for the contrast between these two leaders of Chinese thought remains to the present day. The disciples of Confucius, the so-called "literati," are tinged with their master's agnosticism and insist on the rules of propriety as the best methods of education, while the *Tao Sze,* the believers in the Tao, or divine Reason, are given to philosophical speculation and religious mysticism. The two schools are still divided, and have never effected a conciliation of their differences that might be attained on a common higher ground.

Chwang-tze, one of Lao-tze's disciples, who lived about 330 B. C., has preserved another, an older and more elaborate, report of the meeting between Confucius and the Old Philosopher. Sze-Ma Ch'ien (163-85 B. C.) is sometimes supposed to have derived his account from Chwang-tze, but Chwang-tze's story bears traces of legendary elements which can not but be regarded as fiction, and it is difficult to believe that the historian should have taken his sober sketch from the fantastic tale of a poet-philosopher.

The names of Lao-tze's birthplace, state, province and the locality of his life's work might be considered as invented purposely because of their strange significance if they were not geographically existent. In the first

edition of *Lao-tze's Tao Teh King* we translated Cheu as "the State of Plenty," and will
only add that the word is made up of the
characters "mouth" and "to use," its original
meaning being "to supply everywhere; to
make a circuit all around or everywhere; and
plenty." The Cheu dynasty was so called because the emperor's power reached all over
the civilized world, according to Chinese notions. In the present edition we have pre-
ferred to translate the word Cheu by "the
State of Everywhere."

It would be easy to say that the Old Philosopher was a citizen of Everywhere, and
was born in Good Man's Bend to describe his
innate character; that his home was situated
in Thistle District of Bramble Province to
indicate the poverty and difficulties with
which his life was surrounded.

The plum-tree is the symbol of immortal-
ity, and the ear might signify the man who
was willing to listen. Accordingly Lao-tze's
family name *Li* (plum) seems to be as much
justified as his proper name *Er* (ear). What
splendid material with which to change Lao-
tze into a mythical figure! It is as good as
the life of Napoleon of whom Pérèz made a
solar hero, an Apollo, on account of his name
and the several events of his career—his final
sinking in the west and disappearance on an
island in the Atlantic, the ocean of sunset.
Nevertheless the historicity of Lao-tze and

the authenticity of his book seem to be sufficiently well ascertained.

The historicity of Lao-tze's writing has been doubted only once, but by so great an authority as H. A. Giles. We must, however, remember that the greater part of the Tao Teh King is preserved in quotations in the pre-Christian writings of Lieh-tze, Chwang-tze, and Hwai Nan-tze. (For details see the article in reply to Professor Giles in *The Monist,* XI, pp. 574-601.)

Lao-tze's book on Reason and Virtue first bore the title *Tao Teh.* It was in all outward appearances a mere collection of aphoristic utterances, but full of noble morals and deep meditation. It met the reward which it fully deserved, having by imperial decree been raised to the dignity of canonical authority; hence the name *King* or "canon," completing the title *Tao Teh King,* as now commonly used, which we translate "Canon of Reason and Virtue."

Although Confucian philosophy has become the guiding star of the Chinese government Lao-tze has taken a firm hold on the hearts of the people, and in the progress of time his figure has grown in significance into the stature of a Christ-like superhuman personality. So it happened that later traditions added to Sze-Ma Ch'ien's brief report various details which became more and more fantastic. We learn that Yin Hi, the officer of the frontier, was warned beforehand by astrological science of the sage's coming. He is further reputed to have accompanied his master into the deserts of the west, traveling in a car drawn by black oxen.

Still later legends add to these fables the story of Lao-tze's miraculous conception through the influence of a star, and claim that he was the incarnation of the supreme celestial essence; that he had repeatedly been incarnate, once in the village of the state of Tz'u. This latter birth is represented in analogy with Buddha's nativity, for his mother brought forth the divine child from her left side, and her delivery took place under a tree —in Lao-tze's case it was a plum-tree. The infant at his very birth pointed to the tree saying, "I shall take my surname *Li* (plum) from this tree." His head was white, and his countenance that of an aged man, whence it is said he derived his name Lao-tze, which not only means the Old Philosopher but also the Ancient Child. He is said to have wandered to the farthest extremities of the earth, including the countries Ta Ts'in (which seems to have represented the Roman Empire) and Tu K'ien, where he preached his doctrine and converted the people to the truth. In China he is reported to have helped Wu Wang, the founder of the famous Cheu dynasty, in the year 112 B. C.

Lao-tze's various disciples developed more

and more the mystical elements of Taoism,
the practical application of which terminated
in a belief in alchemy, especially in an elixir
of life.

The Emperor Wu Ti and the emperors of
the T'ang dynasty were staunch believers in
the Old Philosopher. When in the year 666
A. D. Emperor Kao Tsung canonized him he
gave him a rank among the gods as the Great
Supreme (*T'ai Shang*), as the Emperor-God of
the Dark First Cause. Hüan Tsung honored
him in 1013 A. D. with the title *T'ai Shang
Lao Chiün,* the Great Exalted One, the Ancient Master.

We regret to say that the Taoism of China
is a religion which, powerful though it is,
little accords with the venerable old philosopher, and without danger of doing its priests
an injustice may be branded as a system of
superstitions and superstitious practices.

The Taoist church is governed by a Taoist
pope who lives in the splendor of a palace
surrounded by extensive parks near Lung
Hu Shan, scarcely less beautiful than the
garden of the Vatican at Rome.

* * *

Lao-tze's *Tao Teh King* contains so many
surprising analogies with Christian thought
and sentiment, that were its pre-Christian
origin not established beyond the shadow of
a doubt, one would be inclined to discover in
it traces of Christian influence. Not only

does the term *Tao* (word, reason) correspond quite closely to the Greek term *Logos,* but Lao-tze preaches the ethics of requiting hatred with goodness. He insists on the necessity of becoming like unto a little child, of returning to primitive simplicity and purity, of non-assertion and non-resistance, and promises that the crooked shall be straight.

The *Tao Teh King* is brief, but it is filled to the brim with suggestive thoughts.

* * *

Two issues of the author's translation of *Lao-Tze's Tao Teh King* have appeared and two editions of an extract entitled *The Canon of Reason and Virtue.* In the second issue of the first edition of *Lao-Tze's Tao Teh King* attention has been called to misprints in the Chinese text, and alternative readings have been proposed in an additional chapter entitled "Emendations and Comments."

The present edition is meant to be popular and is an enlargement of *The Canon of Reason and Virtue.* Of the larger edition entitled *Lao-Tze's Tao Teh King,* it incorporates the main explanations and the Chinese text which in its revised form we hope is now quite reliable. A few variants which are important for the sense of the text have been added in footnotes. Thus the present little volume being a combination of the larger and the smaller editions, is practically a new work. It contains a comprehensive introduction and incorporates the results of the translator's latest labors in revising and reconsidering the many difficult passages of the *Tao Teh King.* A number of new interpretations flashed upon him from time to time, and some of them will be deemed happy and probably be accepted as final. This certainly is true of the first paragraph of Chapter 2, and also of the second paragraph of Chapter 49.

I do not deem it necessary in this popular edition to introduce controversies or to criticize other translations; nor do I want to correct all the mistakes and misprints of my own former editions. I must be satisfied with offering the best results of my labors. My ideal has been to reproduce the original in a readable form which would be as literal as the difference of languages permits and as intelligible to English-speaking people as is the original to the educated native Chinese. While linguistic obscurities have been removed as much as possible, the sense has upon the whole not been rendered more definite than the original or the traditional interpretation would warrant. Stock phrases which are easily understood, such as "the ten thousand things," meaning the whole world or nature collectively, have been left in their original form; but expressions which without a commentary would be unintelligible, such as "not to depart from the baggage wagon," meaning to preserve one's dignity (Chap. 26), have been replaced by the nearest terms that cover their meaning.

The versification of the quoted poetry is as literal as possible and as simple as in the original. No attempt has been made to improve its literary elegance. The translator was satisfied if he could find a rhyme which would introduce either no change at all in the words or such an indifferent change as would not in the least alter their sense.

The present edition contains also an introduction and comments in which my prior explanations of Lao-tze's thought are restated in a condensed form together with some new observations which in their appropriate places have been incorporated.

The division into chapters as well as the chapter headings were not made by Lao-tze but are the work of later Chinese editors.

I have sought the advice of Mr. Ng Poon Chew, editor of the *Chung Sai Yat Po,* the Chinese daily paper of San Francisco, for the interpretation of some difficult words, and for doubtful passages I deemed a comparison with the Manchu translation desirable, for which purpose I have availed myself of the assistance of Dr. Berthold Laufer of the Field Museum of Chicago.

Prof. Paul Pelliot, of Paris, has recently published in the *T'oung Pao* (1912, pp. 351-430) an account of a Sanskrit translation of the Tao Teh King made in the seventh century for King Kumara of Assam, vassal to the famous Harsha Ciladitya, king of Magadha. Unfortunately this version is lost.

* * *

For further information on Lao-tze the reader is referred to the author's essays *Chinese Philosophy* (Religion of Science Library No. 30), *Chinese Thought,* "The Authenticity of the *Tao Teh King*" (*The Monist,* Vol. XI, pp. 574-601), written in reply to Prof. Herbert A. Giles, "Medhurst's New Translation of the *Tao Teh King*" (*The Open Court,* XX, 174), and the former more complete edition of *Lao-Tze's Tao Teh King.*

This our larger book, entitled *Lao-Tze's Tao Teh King,* which contains a verbatim translation of the Chinese text, has not become entirely antiquated, but we warn students that it stands in need of a revision on the basis of the present emendated edition.

* * *

May this little book fulfil its mission and be a witness to the religious spirit and philosophical depth of a foreign nation whose habits, speech, and dress are strange to us. We are not alone in the world; there are others who search for the truth and are groping after it. Let us become better acquainted with them, let us greet them as brothers, let us understand them and appreciate their ideals!

INTRODUCTION.

A few comments on Lao-tze's favorite expressions will help the reader to understand the drift of his thought.

The character *tao*[1] being composed of the characters "moving on" and "head," depicts a "going ahead." The original meaning of the word is "way" in the same sense as in English, denoting both "path" and "method."

The same association of ideas prevails in almost all languages. The Greek word *methodos*[2] is a derivative of *hodos*[3] "path" (combined with the preposition *meta,* "according to," "after") and so "method" too originally means "way" or rather "according to a way." In the sense of method the word Tao acquires the significance of "principle, rational-

---

[1] 道   [2] μέθοδος.   [3] ὁδός.

ity, or reason," then "the right **way**," or
"truth," the *Urvernunft* of German mystics. Finally Tao comes to possess the
meaning of "rational speech" or "word,"
and in this sense it closely resembles the
Greek *Logos,* for in addition to its philosophical significance the term **Tao**
touches a religious chord in the souls
of the Chinese just as did the word
Logos among the Platonists and the
Greek Christians. The term Tao denotes "word" and also "way" in the same
religious sense in which they are used
in the New Testament: the former in
the first verse of the Fourth Gospel, "In
the beginning was the *word*"; and the
latter in the saying of Christ, "I am the
way, the *truth*, and the life" (John xiv.
6). In both passages the word Tao is
the right term by which to translate
"word," "way," and "truth."

The Tao of man, *jan tao*,[4] is the process of ratiocination, and as such it is
fallible; but there is an Eternal Reason,
ch'ang tao,[5] also called *t'ien tao*,[6] "Heav-

[4] 人道   [5] 常道   [6] 天道

en's Reason," i. e., the world-order which
shapes all things, and the burden of
Lao-tze's message is to let this Heaven's
Reason or Eternal Reason prevail. The
man who is guided by the Eternal Reason is the master, *chiün*;[7] the superior
thinker, *chiün tze*;[8] he is the holy man,
shan jan;[9] the man of Reason, *yin tao
che*[10] or *tung yü tao che*;[11] and the man
of truth, *chen jan*.[12]

We translate Tao by "Reason," and we
capitalize the word in order to remind
the reader that it is not the reason of the
rationalist, nor the rationality of argument, but the universal world-order, or
in other words, the eternal Reason of
the divine dispensation, the Logos, to
which man looks up with reverence.

The second word of the title, *Teh*,[13]
"virtue," which, strange enough, Legge
translates "attribute," is made up of
characters meaning "man," "heart" and

[7] 君   [8] 君子   [9] 聖人

[10] Literally, "having Reason the one."
[11] Literally, "identified with Reason the
one."

[12] 眞人   [13] 德

"straight." It denotes man's straightness of heart.

The favorite phrase of Lao-tze's ethics, which furnishes a key to his mode
of thought, reads *wei wu wei*, (爲 無 爲)
"act non-act," and we have commonly
translated the words by "act with non-
assertion."

The Chinese *wei* means not only "to
do something," but also "to act" as on
the stage, or "to make a show, to show
off, to pose, to parade oneself." The
phrase *wei wu wei* might be translated
"to do without ado" or "to act without
acting" (viz., without posing), were it
not for the fact that the moral element
is uppermost in Lao-tze's mind. He denounces the vanity of self-display and
egotism, and so we believe that *wei wu
wei* is best rendered by "acting with
non-assertion." The meaning is clear
through the context, and there is no
need of interpreting Lao-tze's words
either in a mystical or a quietist sense.

There are three negatives in Chinese:
pu, "not," the simple negation *wu* "lacking in, non-existent, without"; and *fei,*

"by no means." Though we can not lay
down a general rule about their distinc-
tions, there are different shades of meaning according to the context which we
have tried to bring out in our English
version. Sometimes the meaning of the
negated word, or the ironic sense in
which it is used, influences the negative. In Chapter 49 *pu shan*, "ungood-
ness", means "evil," but in Chapter 38,
pu teh, "unvirtue," means that higher
virtue which makes no show and does
not even assume the name. In Chapter
57 *wu shi*, "non-diplomacy," is that
higher mode of statesmanship with
which a good ruler will unostentatiously
govern the empire. On the other hand
Lao-tze speaks of both *fei tao*, i. e., "lack
of reason" or "anti-reason" (Chapter 53)
and *pu tao* (Chapters 30 and 55) "un-
reason," which soon ceases, while "the
reason that can be reasoned" (*tao ko tao*)
is declared to be "by no means the eternal Reason (*fei ch'ang tao*)."

The term *wu*, "non-existence" (Chapter 40), is not annihilation but denotes
absence of concrete particularity or of

materiality. It is intended to describe what we would call the purely formal, including purely formal thought, viz., the prototypes of things as well as ideals. Materiality makes things real but non-materiality,[14] as set forth in Chapter 11, while giving shape to things by cutting away certain portions, renders them useful.

Lao-tze's appreciation of oneness is to be expected of a philosopher of the Tao, of Divine Reason. He speaks of oneness[15] as giving character to things that are units (Chapter 39) and unity cannot be disintegrated (Chapter 10).

Lao-tze's reference to trinity as begetting all things (Chapter 42) is, to say the least, curious, perhaps profound, and

[14] For the meaning of "nought" in Oriental thought see the author's *Foundations of Mathematics*, pp. 134ff. Compare also on the significance of non-realities the article "Mysticism" in *The Monist*, Vol. XVIII, p. 86; further, *Buddhism and Its Christian Critics*, pp. 110, 119ff. and 218, where Goethe is quoted on nothingness.

[15] For the connection of Oneness with Quality see the author's *Personality*, pp. 36-38, and "The Significance of Quality," *Monist*, XV, 375. Cf. *The Phiolsophy of Form*, pp. 12-13.

Christians will also be interested in the idea that the Son of Heaven as the High Priest of the people must bear the sins of mankind (Chapter 78).

Lao-tze's style is characterized by paradox as in "do without ado" (commonly translated "act with non-assertion" as in Chapters 2, 3, 10, etc.); "know the unknowable," "be sick of sickness"(Chapter 71); "practice non-practice," "taste the tasteless" (Chapter 63); "marching without marching" (Chapter 69). Similarly the phrases "the form of the formless"[16] and "the image of the imageless"[17] (Chapter 14) etc. are used to describe what Kant calls "pure form," i. e., non-material or ideal forms such as geometrical figures, and which corresponds to the Buddhist term *arupo*, "the formless," in the sense of "the bodiless."

Undoubtedly the best sayings of Laotze are: "Requite hatred with goodness[18] (Chapter 63); and "The good I meet with goodness; the bad I also meet with

[16] 無狀之狀   [17] 無象之象
[18] 報怨以德 (Literally, "with virtue.")

goodness[19]. . . . The faithful I meet with faith, the faithless I also meet with faith" (Chapter 49).

Other remarkable ideas of Lao-tze are his preference for simplicity (Chapters 17, 28, 37, 57), for purity (Chapter 45), for emptiness (Chapters 3, 4, 5), for rest and peace[20] (Chapter 31), for silence (Chapters 2, 23, 43, 56), for tenderness (Chapters 52, 76, 78), especially the tenderness of water (Chapter 78), for weakness (Chapters 36, 40) for compassion (Chapter 67), for lowliness or humility (Chapter 61), for thrift (Chapter 59), for returning home to the Tao (Chapters 25, 40), for spontaneity or lack of effort (Chapter 6), etc.

He is against restrictions and prohibitions as producing disorder (Chapter

[19] 善者吾善之 不善者吾亦善之

[20] Lao-tze uses no less than eight synonyms for "rest" or "quietude": (1) *t'ien tan,* "quietude and peace," Chap. 31; (2) *tsing,* "quietude," Chaps. 16, 26, 37, 45, 61; (3) *ngan,* "still," Chap. 15, and "rest", Chap. 35; (4) *p'ing,* "contentment," Chap. 35; (5) *t'ai,* "comfort," Chap. 35; (6) *tsan,* "calm," Chap. 4; (7) *tsih,* "calm," Chap. 25; (8) *yen,* "calmly," Chap. 26.

57), against ostentation (Chapter 58), against learnedness as unwisdom (Chapter 81). He believes that the Tao when sought is found (Chapter 62), and he praises the state of a little child (Chapters 10, 28, 55). He compares himself to a babe (Chapter 20) and calls himself the child or son of the Tao and the Tao his mother (Chapter 52); on the other hand the sage looks upon the people as children (Chapter 49).

Heaven's impartiality[21] (Chapter 79) which shows no preference to favorites is expected of the sage by Lao-tze who praises the emptiness of heaven (Chapter 5), the lowliness of the valley (Chapters 32, 39, 41, 66), and the stretching of the bow which brings down the high and raises the low (Chapter 77), etc.

Though the Tao, being an abstract philosophical principle, seems to leave no room for a belief in God, Lao-tze refers repeatedly to God, first identifying God with Reason as "the arch-father of the ten thousand things," (Chapter 4), and then he speaks of Reason as pre-

[21] **Compare** with this Matt. v. 45.

ceding even "the Lord" (Chapter 4). In
Chapter 70 he calls the Tao "the ancestor of words" and "the master of deeds"
which also personifies Reason. The passage where he speaks of "the father of
the doctrine" (Chapter 42) may be doubtful, for the commentators explain it to
mean "the foundation of the doctrine";
but the idea of calling the Tao the father
of truth is not contrary to Lao-tze's
thought, for he speaks of the Tao twice
as the "mother" (Chapters 20 and 52)
and once as "the world's mother" (Chapter 52). In Chapter 74, when referring
to divine justice cutting short the lives
of men, the Tao is compared to "the
great carpenter who hews." All these
passages are figures of speech, but are
not the Christian ideas of God as a Lord,
as a father, as an architect (as the Free-
masons have it), also allegories?

老子道德經

游者可以爲綸飛者可以爲矰。至於龍吾不能知其乘風雲而上天吾

弟子曰鳥吾知其能飛。魚吾知其能游獸吾知其能走。走者可以爲罔

欲態色與淫志是皆無益於子之身吾所以告子若是而已。孔子去謂

累而行。吾聞之良賈深藏若虛君子盛德容貌若愚。去子之驕氣多

其人與骨皆已朽矣獨其言在耳。且君子得其時則駕不得其時則蓬

曰聃。周守藏室之史也。孔子適周將問禮於老子。老子曰子所言者。

司馬遷曰　老子者楚苦縣厲鄉曲仁里人也。姓李氏名耳字伯陽諡

司馬遷史記老子傳

老子乃著書上下篇言道德之意五千餘言而去莫知其所終。

之見周之衰乃遂去至關　關令尹喜曰子將隱矣彊爲我著書　於是

今日見老子其猶龍邪。　老子修道德其學以自隱無名爲務。　居周久

老子道德經

上篇

第一章　體道

道可道。非常道。名可名。非常名。無名天地之始。有名萬物之母。故常無欲以觀其妙。常有欲以觀其徼。此兩者同出。而異名。同謂之玄。玄之又玄。眾妙之門。

第二章　養身

天下皆知美之爲美。斯惡已。皆知善之爲善。斯不善已。故有無相生。難易相成。長短相形。高下相傾。音聲相和。前後相隨。是以道冲而用之。或不盈。淵乎似萬物之宗。挫其銳。解其紛。和其光。

第四章　無源

知無欲使夫知者不敢爲也。爲無爲則無不治。

不亂是以聖人之治虛其心。實其腹。弱其志。強其骨。常使民無

不尙賢使民不爭。不貴難得之貨。使民不爲盜。不見可欲。使心

第三章　安民

而不恃功成而弗居。夫惟不居。是以弗去。

聖人處無爲之事行不言之敎。萬物作焉而不辭生而不有爲

天長地久。天地所以能長且久者。以其不自生。故能長生。是以

第七章　韜光

谷神不死。是謂玄牝。玄牝之門。是謂天地根。綿綿若存。用之不勤。

第六章　成象

其猶橐籥乎。虛而不屈。動而愈出。多言數窮。不如守中。

天地不仁。以萬物爲芻狗。聖人不仁。以百姓爲芻狗。天地之間。

第五章　虛用

同其塵。湛兮似若存。吾不知誰之子。象帝之先。

持而盈之不如其已。揣而銳之。不可長保。金玉滿堂。莫之能守。

第九章　運夷

無尤。

地。心善淵。與善仁。言善信。政善治。事善能。動善時。夫惟不爭。故

上善若水。水善利萬物而不爭。處眾人之所惡。故幾于道。居善

第八章　易性

私。

聖人後其身而身先。外其身而身存。非以其無私邪。故能成其

用。

用。鑿戶牖以爲室。當其無。有室之用。故有之以爲利。無之以爲

三十輻共一轂。當其無。有車之用。埏埴以爲器。當其無。有器之

第十一章　無用

而不有。爲而不恃。長而不宰。是謂玄德。

治國能無爲。天門開闔能爲雌。明白四達。能無知。生之畜之。生

載營魄抱一。能無離。專氣致柔。能嬰兒。滌除玄覽。能無疵。愛民

第十章　能爲

富貴而驕。自遺其咎。功成名遂。身退。天之道。

愛以身爲天下者。則可以託天下。

有身。及吾無身。吾有何患。故貴以身爲天下者。則可以寄天下。

若驚。是謂寵辱若驚。何謂貴大患若身。吾所以有大患者。爲吾

寵辱若驚。貴大患若身。何謂寵辱若驚。寵爲下。得之若驚。失之

　　第十三章　厭恥

此。

心發狂。難得之貨。令人行妨。是以聖人爲腹。不爲目。故去彼取

五色令人目盲。五音令人耳聾。五味令人口爽。馳騁田獵。令人

　　第十二章　檢欲

第十四章　贊玄

視之不見名曰夷。聽之不聞名曰希。搏之不得。名曰微。此三者不可致詰。故混而爲一。其上不皦。其下不昧。繩繩兮不可名。復歸于無物。是謂無狀之狀。無象之象。是謂惚恍。迎之不見其首。隨之不見其後。執古之道。以御今之有。以知古始。是謂道紀。

第十五章　顯德

古之善爲士者微妙玄通。深不可識。夫惟不可識。故強爲之容。與兮若冬涉川。猶兮若畏四隣。儼兮其若客。渙兮若冰之將釋。

太上下不知有之。其次。親之譽之。其次畏之。其次。侮之。故信不

第十七章 淳風

容容乃公。公乃王。王乃天。天乃道。道乃久没身不殆。

歸根曰靜。是謂復命。復命曰常。知常曰明。不知常妄作凶。知常

致虛極。守靜篤。萬物并作吾以觀其復。夫物芸芸。各復歸其根。

第十六章 歸根

能安以動之徐生。保此道不欲盈。夫惟不盈。故能弊不新成。

敦兮其若樸。曠兮其若谷。渾兮其若濁。孰能濁以靜之徐清。孰

絕學無憂。唯之與阿。相去幾何。善之與惡。相去何若。人之所畏。

第二十章　異俗

此三者以為文不足。故令有所屬。見素抱樸。少私寡欲。

絕聖棄智。民利百倍。絕仁棄義。民復孝慈。絕巧棄利。盜賊無有。

第十九章　還淳

忠信。

大道廢。有仁義。智慧出。有大偽。六親不和。有孝慈。國家昏亂。有

第十八章　俗薄

足焉。有不信。猶兮其貴言。功成事遂。百姓皆謂我自然。

兮惚。其中有物。窈兮冥兮。其中有精。其精甚眞。其中有信。自古

孔德之容。惟道是從。道之爲物。惟恍惟惚。惚兮恍。其中有象。恍

第二十一章　虛心

頑且鄙。我獨異于人。而貴求食於母。

察察。我獨悶悶。忽兮若海。漂兮若無所止。衆人皆有以。而我獨

我獨若遺我愚人之心也哉。沌沌兮。俗人昭昭。我獨若昏。俗人

泊兮其未兆。如嬰兒之未孩。乘乘兮。若無所歸。衆人皆有餘。而

不可不畏荒兮其未央哉。衆人熙熙。如享大牢。如春登臺。我獨

希言自然飄風不終朝驟雨不終日。孰爲此者。天地。天地尚不

第二十三章　虛無

哉誠全而歸之。

長。夫惟不爭。故天下莫能與之爭。古之所謂曲則全者豈虛言

爲天下式。不自見。故明。不自是。故彰。不自伐。故有功。不自矜。故

曲則全枉則直窪則盈弊則新。少則得。多則惑。是以聖人抱一。

第二十二章　益謙

及今其名不去。以閱衆甫吾何以知衆甫之然哉。以此。

能久。而況于人乎故從事于道者道者同于道從事于德者同

于德從*事*于失*者同于失同于道者道亦樂得之同于德者德

亦樂得之同于失者失亦樂得之。信不足焉。有不信。

第二十四章　苦恩

跂者不立跨者不行。自見者不明。自是者不彰。自伐者無功。自

矜者不長其于道也曰餘食贅行物或惡之。故有道者不處也。

第二十五章　象玄

有物混成。先天地生寂兮寥兮。獨立而不改。周行而不殆可以

* These characters are omitted in most editions.

† These characters are repeated by Fu Yi of the Tang according to Pi Yüan.

爲天下母。吾不知其名。字之曰道。強爲名之曰大。大曰逝。逝曰遠。遠曰反。故道大。天大。地大。王亦大。域中有四大。而王居其一。焉人法地。地法天。天法道。道法自然。

第二十六章　重德

重爲輕根。靜爲躁君。是以聖人終日行。不離輜重*。雖有榮觀。燕處超然。奈何萬乘之主。而以身輕天下。輕則失臣。躁則失君。

* Here the Lin H'i Yih edition reads 靜 for 輜.

第二十七章　巧用

善行無轍迹。善言無瑕讁。善計無籌策。善閉無關鍵而不可開。

器。聖人用之則爲官長。故大制不割。

榮。守其辱。爲天下谷。爲天下谷，常德乃足。復歸于朴。朴散則爲

其白。守其黑。爲天下式。爲天下式，常德不忒。復歸于無極。知其

知其雄。守其雌。爲天下谿。爲天下谿，常德不離。復歸于嬰兒。知

第二十八章　反樸

之資。不貴其師。不愛其資。雖智 大迷。是謂要妙。

物。故無棄物。是謂襲明。故善人者。不善人之師。不善人者。善人

善結無繩約。而不可解。是以聖人常善救人。故無棄人。常善救

道早已。

勿伐果而無驕。果而不得已。果而勿强。物壯則老。是謂不道。不
大軍之後必有凶年。善者果而已。不敢以取强。果而勿矜。果而
以道佐人主者不以兵强天下。其事好還。師之所處荊棘生焉。

第三十章　儉武

是以聖人去甚。去奢。去泰。

敗之。執者失之。故物或行。或隨。或呴。或吹。或强。或羸。或載。或隳。

將欲取天下而爲之。吾見其不得已。天下神器不可爲也。爲者

第二十九章　無爲

道常無名。樸雖小。天下不敢臣。侯王若能守。萬物將自賓。天地

第三十二章　聖德

上勢。則以喪禮處之。殺人衆多。以悲哀泣之。戰勝以喪禮處之。

于天下矣。吉事尚左。凶事尚右。偏將軍居左。上將軍居右。言居

上。勝而不美。而美之者。是樂殺人。夫樂殺人者。則不可以得志

兵則貴右。兵者不祥之器。非君子之器。不得已而用之。恬淡爲

夫佳兵不祥之器。物或惡之。故有道者不處。君子居則貴左。用

第三十一章　偃武

大。是以聖人終不爲大。故能成其大。

萬物。而不爲主。常無欲。可名于小。萬物歸焉。而不爲主。可名爲

大道氾兮。其可左右。萬物恃之以生。而不辭。功成不名有。愛養

第三十四章　任成

有志。不失其所者久。死而不亡者壽。

知人者智。自知者明。勝人者有力。自勝者強。知足者富。強行者

第三十三章　辨德

知止。知止所以不殆。譬道之在天下。猶川谷之於江海也。

相合。以降甘露。民莫之令。而自均。始制有名。名亦既有。夫亦將

道常無爲。而無不爲。侯王若能守。萬物將自化。化而欲作。吾將

第三十七章　爲政

之利器不可以示人。

將欲奪之。必固與之。是謂微明。柔弱勝剛強。魚不可脫于淵。國

將欲歙之。必固張之。將欲弱之。必固強之。將欲廢之。必固與之。

第三十六章　微明

乎其無味。視之不足見。聽之不足聞。用之不可既。

執大象。天下往。往而不害。安平泰。樂與餌。過客止。道之出口。淡

第三十五章　仁德

不居其華。故去彼取此。

識者道之華而愚之始。是以大丈夫處其厚。不居其薄。處其實。

后仁失仁而后義。失義而后禮。夫禮者。忠信之薄。而亂之首。前

爲。上禮爲之而莫之應。則攘臂而仍之。故失道而后德。失德而

爲。下德爲之而有以爲。上仁爲之而無以爲。上義爲之而有以

上德不德。是以有德。下德不失德。是以無德。上德無爲而無以

第三十八章　論德

下篇

鎮之以無名之朴。無名之朴亦將不欲。不欲以靜天下將自定。

反者道之動。弱者道之用。天地萬物生于有。有生于無。

第四十章　去用

非乎。故致數車無車。不欲琭琭如玉。落落如石。

爲本。高以下爲基。是以侯王自謂孤寡不穀。此其以賤爲本耶。

竭。萬物無以生將恐滅。侯王無以正。而貴高。將恐蹶。故貴以賤

清。將恐裂。地無以寧。將恐發。神無以靈。將恐歇。谷無以盈。將恐

盈。萬物得一以生。侯王得一以爲天下正。其致之一也。天無以

昔之得一者。天得一以清。地得一以寧。神得一以靈。谷得一以

第三十九章　法本

第四十一章　同異

上士聞道勤而行之。中士聞道若存若亡。下士聞道大笑之。不笑不足以爲道故建言者有之。明道若昧進道若退夷道若類。上德若谷大白若辱廣德若不足建德若偷質貞若渝大方無隅。大器晚成。大音希聲。大象無形道隱無名夫唯道善貸且成。

第四十二章　道化

道生一。一生二。二生三。三生萬物。萬物負陰而抱陽冲氣以爲和。人之所惡唯孤寡不穀而王公以爲稱故或損之而益或益之而損。人之所教我亦教之。強梁者不得其死吾將以爲敎父。

大辯若訥。躁勝寒。靜勝熱。清淨爲天下正。

大成若缺其用不弊。大盈若冲。其用不窮。大直若屈大巧若拙。

第四十五章　洪德

亡。知足不辱。知止不殆可以長久。

名與身孰親。身與貨孰多。得與亡孰病。甚愛必大費多藏必厚

第四十四章　立戒

有益不言之教。無爲之益天下希及之。

天下之至柔。馳騁天下之至堅。無有入無間。吾是以知無爲之

第四十三章　偏用

天下。常以無事。及有事不足以取天下。

為學日益。為道日損。損之又損。以至于無為。無為而無不為。取

不行而知。不見而名。不為而成。

不出戶知天下。不窺牖見天道。其出彌遠。其知彌少。是以聖人

禍莫大于不知足。咎莫大于欲得。故知足之足。常足。

天下有道。却走馬以糞。天下無道。戎馬生于郊。罪莫大于可欲。

夫何故以其無死地。

入軍不避甲兵兕無所投其角。虎無所措其爪。兵無所容其双。

十有三夫何故以其生生之厚。蓋聞善攝生者陸行不遇兕虎。

出生入死生之徒十有三死之徒十有三人之生動之死地亦

第五十章　貴生

天下。渾其心。百姓皆注其耳目聖人皆孩之。

德*善信者吾信之。不信者吾亦信之。德信聖人在天下慄慄爲

聖人無常心。以百姓之心爲心。善者吾善之。不善者吾亦善之。

第四十九章　任德

*Here the Lin H'i Yih edition reads 得 for 德

見小曰明守柔曰強用其光復歸其明。無遺身殃。是謂習常。

母沒身不殆塞其兌閉其門。終身不勤開其兌濟其事。終身不

天下有始以爲天下母。旣知其母復知其子旣知其子復守其

第五十二章　　歸元

成之。熟之。養之。覆之。生而不有。爲而不恃長而不宰。是謂玄德。

之尊德之貴夫莫之命而常自然故道生之德畜之長之育之。

道生之德畜之。物形之。勢成之。是以萬物莫不尊道而貴德道

第五十一章　養德

觀國以天下觀天下吾何以知天下之然哉以此。

修之于天下其德乃普故以身觀身以家觀家以鄉觀鄉以國

修之于家其德有餘修之于鄉其德乃長修之于國其德乃豐

善建者不拔善抱者不脫子孫祭祀不輟修之于身其德乃眞。

第五十四章　修觀

非道哉。

除田甚蕪倉甚虛服文綵帶利劒厭飮食財貨有餘是謂盜夸。

使我介然有知行于大道唯施是畏大道甚夷而民好徑朝甚

第五十三章　益證

不可得而害。不可得而貴。亦不可得而賤。故爲天下貴。

其塵。是謂玄同。故不可得而親。亦不可得而踈。不可得而利。亦

知者不言。言者不知。塞其兌。閉其門。挫其銳。解其紛。和其光。同

第五十六章　玄德

謂之不道。不道早已。

之至也。知和曰常。知常曰明。益生曰祥。心使氣曰强。物壯將老。

而握固。未知牝牡之合而朘作。精之至也。終日號而嗌不嗄。和

含德之厚。比于赤子。毒蟲不螫。猛獸不據。玃鳥不搏。骨弱筋柔

第五十五章　玄符

固久。是以聖人方而不割。廉而不劌。直而不肆。光而不耀。

禍之所伏。孰知其極。其無正。正復為奇。善復為妖。人之迷其日

其政悶悶。其民醇醇。其政察察。其民缺缺。禍兮福之所倚。福兮

第五十八章　順化

自正。我無事。而民自富。我無欲。而民自樸。

法令滋彰。盜賊多有。故聖人云。我無為而民自化。我好靜。而民

下多忌諱。而民彌貧。民多利器。國家滋昏。人多技巧。奇物滋起。

以正治國。以奇用兵。以無事取天下。吾何以知其然哉。以此。天

第五十七章　淳風

大國者下流。天下之交。天下之牝。牝常以靜勝牡。以靜爲下。故

第六十一章　謙德

治大國若烹小鮮。以道莅天下。其鬼不神。非其鬼不神。其神不

傷人。非其神不傷人。聖人亦不傷人。夫兩不相傷。故德交歸焉。

第六十章　居位

可以長久。是謂深根固蔕。長生久視之道。

則無不剋。無不剋則莫知其極。莫知其極。可以有國。有國之母。

治人事天。莫若嗇。夫惟嗇是謂早服。早服謂之重積德。重積德

第五十九章　守道

罪以免耶。故爲天下貴。

駟馬不如坐進此道。古之所以貴此道者何也。不曰求以得有
以加人人之不善何棄之有。故立天子置三公。雖有拱璧以先
道者萬物之奧。善人之寶。不善人之所保。美言可以市。尊行可

第六十二章　爲道

各得其所欲。大者宜爲下。

取。或下而取。大國不過欲兼畜人。小國不過欲入事人。夫兩者
大國以下小國則取小國。小國以下大國則取大國。故或下以

于足下。爲者敗之。執者失之。聖人無爲。故無敗。無執。故無失。民

于未亂。合抱之木生于毫末。九層之臺起于累土。千里之行。始

其安易持其未兆易謀。其脆易破。其微易散。爲之于未有治之

第六十四章　守微

難之故終無難。

不爲大故能成其大。夫輕諾必寡信。多易必多難。是以聖人猶

于其細。天下難事必作于易天下大事必作于細。是以聖人終

爲無爲。事無事。味無味。大小多少。報怨以德。圖難于其易。爲大

第六十三章　思始

江海所以能爲百谷王者。以其善下之。故能爲百谷王。是以聖

第六十六章　後己

是謂玄德。玄德深矣遠矣與物反矣乃至于大順。

治國國之賊。不以智治國國之福。知此兩者亦楷式。常知楷式。

古之善爲道者。非以明民將以愚之。民之難治以其智多。以智

第六十五章　淳德

不敢爲。

欲不貴難得之貨。學不學復衆人之所過以輔萬物之自然。而

之從事常于幾成而敗之。愼終如始則無敗事。是以聖人欲不

之。

廣。捨後且先。死矣。夫慈以戰則勝。以守則固。天將救之。以慈衞

勇。儉故能廣。不敢爲天下先。故能成器長。今捨慈且勇。捨儉且

有三寶。持而寶之。一曰慈。二曰儉。三曰不敢爲天下先。慈故能

天下皆謂我大似不肖。夫惟大。故似不肖。若肖久矣其細。夫我

第六十七章　三寶

下莫能與之爭。

民不重。處前而民不害。是以天下樂推而不厭以其不爭。故天

人欲上民。必以言下之。欲先民。必以身後之。是以聖人處上而

吾言甚易知。甚易行。天下莫能知。莫能行。言有宗。事有君。夫唯

第七十章　知難

相加。衰*者勝矣。

攘無臂。仍無敵。執無兵。禍莫大于輕敵。輕敵幾喪吾寶。故抗兵

用兵有言吾不敢爲主。而爲客。不敢進寸。而退尺。是謂行無行。

第六十九章　玄用

謂不爭之德。是謂用人之力。是謂配天。古之極。

善爲士者不武。善戰者不怒。善勝敵者不爭。善用人者爲下。是

第六十八章　配天

*Here the Lin H'i
Yih edition reads
衰 for 衰

勇于敢則殺勇于不敢則活。此兩者或利或害。天之所惡。孰知

第七十三章　任爲

不厭是以聖人自知不自見。自愛不自貴。故去彼取此。

民不畏威大威至矣。無狹其所居。無厭其所生。夫唯不厭。是以

第七十二章　愛己

是以不病。

知不知上。不知知病。夫唯病病。是以不病。聖人不病。以其病病。

第七十一章　知病

無知。是以不我知。知我者希。則我貴。是以聖人被褐懷玉。

民之饑。以其上食稅之多。是以饑。民之難治。以其上之有爲。

第七十五章　貪損

大匠斲者希有不傷手矣。

殺之。孰敢常有司殺者殺。夫代司殺者殺。是謂代大匠斲。夫代

民不畏死。奈何以死懼之。若使民常畏死。而爲奇者吾得執而

第七十四章　制惑

而自來。繟然而善謀。天網恢恢。疎而不失。

其故。是以聖人猶難之。天之道不爭而善勝。不言而善應不召

與之。天之道。損有餘而補不足。人之道則不然。損不足以奉有

天之道。其猶張弓乎。高者抑之。下者擧之。有餘者損之。不足者

第七十七章　天道

共。強大處下柔弱處上。

槁。故堅強者死之徒。柔弱者生之徒。是以兵強則不勝。木強則

人之生也柔弱。其死也堅強。萬物草木之生也柔脆。其死也枯

第七十六章　戒強

者。是賢于貴生。

是以難治民之輕死以其求生之厚。是以輕死。夫唯無以生為

德司契。無德司徹。天道無親。常與善人。

和大怨。必有餘怨。安以爲善是以聖人執左契。而不責于人。有

第七十九章　任契

社稷主。受國之不祥。是謂天下王。正言若反。

勝强柔之勝剛。天下莫不知莫能行。故聖人云。受國之垢。是謂

天下柔弱莫過于水。而攻堅强者莫之能勝。其無以易之。弱之

第七十八章　任信

不處其不欲見賢耶。

餘執能有餘以奉天下。唯有道者是以聖人爲而不恃功成而

害。聖人之道為而不爭。

聖人不積。既以為人己愈有。既以與人己愈多。天之道利而不

信言不美美言不信。善者不辯。辯者不善。知者不博。博者不知。

　第八十一章　顯質

不相往來。

食美其服。安其居。樂其俗。鄰國相望雞狗之聲相聞。民至老死。

舟輿。無所乘之。雖有甲兵。無所陳之。使民復結繩而用之。甘其

小國寡民。使有什伯人之器。而不用。使民重死而不遠徙。雖有

　第八十章　獨立

老君

THE OLD PHILOSOPHER'S CANON
OF REASON AND VIRTUE.

SZE-MA-CH'IEN ON LAO-TZE.

Lao-tze was born in the hamlet Ch'ü-Jan (Good Man's Bend), Li - Hsiang (Grinding County), K'u-Hien (Thistle District), of Ch'u (Bramble land). His family was the Li gentry (*Li* meaning Plum). His proper name was Er (Ear), his posthumous title Po-Yang (Prince Positive), his appellation Tan (Long-lobed). In Cheu (the State of Everywhere) he was in charge of the secret archives as state historian.

Confucius went to Cheu in order to consult Lao-tze on the rules of propriety.

[When Confucius, speaking of propriety, praised the sages of antiquity], Lao-tze said: "The men of whom you speak, Sir, together with their bones, have mouldered. Their words alone are

still extant. If a noble man finds his
time he rises, but if he does not find
his time he drifts like a roving-plant
and wanders about. I observe that the
wise merchant hides his treasures deeply
as if he were poor. The noble man of
perfect virtue assumes an attitude as
though he were stupid. Let go, Sir,
your proud airs, your many wishes, your
affection and exaggerated plans. All
this is of no use to you, Sir. That is
what I have to communicate to you,
and that is all."

Confucius left. [Unable to understand
Lao-tze], he addressed his disciples, saying: "I know that the birds can fly, I
know that the fishes can swim, I know
that the wild animals can run. For the
running, one could make nooses; for the
swimming, one could make nets; for the
flying, one could make arrows. As to the
dragon I cannot know how he can be-
stride wind and clouds when he heaven-
ward rises. To-day I saw Lao-tze. Is
he perhaps like the dragon?"

Lao-tze practised Reason and virtue.

His doctrine aims at self-concealment and namelessness.

Lao-tze resided in Cheu most of his life. When he foresaw the decay of Cheu, he departed and came to the frontier. The custom house officer Yin-Hi said: "Sir, since it pleases you to retire, I request you for my sake to write a book."

Thereupon Lao-tze wrote a book of two parts consisting of five thousand and odd words, in which he discussed the concepts of Reason and virtue. Then he departed.

No one knows where he died.

THE OLD PHILOSOPHER'S CANON OF REASON AND VIRTUE.

I.

1. REASON'S REALIZATION.

1. The Reason that can be reasoned is not the eternal Reason. The name that can be named is not the eternal Name. The Unnamable is of heaven and earth the beginning. The Namable becomes of the ten thousand things the mother.

Therefore it is said:

2. "He who desireless is found
The spiritual of the world will sound.
But he who by desire is bound
Sees the mere shell of things around."

3. These two things are the same in source but different in name. Their sameness is called a mystery. Indeed,

it is the mystery of mysteries. Of all
spirituality it is the door.

2. SELF-CULTURE.

1. Everywhere it is obvious that if
beauty makes a display of beauty, it is
sheer ugliness. It is obvious that if
goodness makes a display of goodness,
it is sheer badness. For

2. "To be and not to be are mutually con-
    ditioned.
    The difficult, the easy, are mutually
    definitioned.
    The long, the short, are mutually ex-
    hibitioned.
    Above, below, are mutually cogni-
    tioned.
    The sound, the voice, are mutually
    coalitioned.
    Before and after are mutually posi-
    tioned."

3. Therefore
The holy man abides by non-assertion
in his affairs and conveys by silence his
instruction. When the ten thousand
things arise, verily, he refuses them not.

He quickens but owns not. He acts
but claims not. Merit he accomplishes,
but he does not dwell on it.

> "Since he does not dwell on it
> It will never leave him."

3. KEEPING THE PEOPLE QUIET.

1. Not boasting of one's worth fore-
stalls people's envy.
Not prizing treasures difficult to obtain keeps people from committing theft.

2. Not contemplating what kindles desire keeps the heart unconfused.

3. Therefore the holy man when he
governs empties the people's hearts but
fills their stomachs. He weakens their
ambition but strengthens their bones.
Always he keeps the people unsophisticated and without desire. He causes
that the crafty do not dare to act. When
he acts with non-assertion there is nothing ungoverned.

4. SOURCELESS.

1. Reason is empty, but its use is inexhaustible. In its profundity, verily, it

resembleth the arch-father of the ten thousand things.

    2. "It will blunt its own sharpness,
        Will its tangles adjust;
        It will dim its own radiance
        And be one with its dust."

    3. Oh, how calm it seems to remain! I know not whose son it is. Apparently even the Lord it precedes.

5. THE FUNCTION OF EMPTINESS.

    1. But for heaven and earth's humaneness, the ten thousand things are straw dogs. But for the holy man's humaneness, the hundred families are straw dogs.

    2. Is not the space between heaven and earth like unto a bellows? It is empty; yet it collapses not. It moves, and more and more comes forth. [But]

    3. "How soon exhausted is
        A gossip's fulsome talk!
        And should we not prefer
        On the middle path to walk?"

6. THE COMPLETION OF FORM.

1. "The valley spirit not expires,
Mysterious woman 'tis called by the sires.
The mysterious woman's door, to boot,
Is called of heaven and earth the root.
Forever and aye it seems to endure
And its use is without effort sure."

7. DIMMING RADIANCE.

1. Heaven endures and earth is lasting. And why can heaven and earth endure and be lasting? Because they do not live for themselves. On that account can they endure.

2. Therefore
The holy man puts his person behind and his person comes to the front. He surrenders his person and his person is preserved. Is it not because he seeks not his own? For that reason he can accomplish his own.

8. EASY BY NATURE.

1. Superior goodness resembleth water. The water's goodness benefiteth the ten thousand things, yet it quarreleth not.

2. Water dwelleth in the places which the multitudes of men shun; therefore it is near unto the eternal Reason

3. The dwelling of goodness is in lowliness. The heart of goodness is in commotion. When giving, goodness showeth benevolence. In words, goodness keepeth faith. In government goodness standeth for order. In business goodness exhibiteth ability. The movements of goodness keep time.

4. It quarreleth not. Therefore it is not rebuked.

9. PRACTISING PLACIDITY.

1. Grasp to the full, are you not likely foiled? Scheme too sharply, can you wear long? If gold and jewels fill the hall no one can protect it.

2. Rich and high but proud, brings about its own doom. To accomplish merit and acquire fame, then to withdraw, that is Heaven's Way.

10. WHAT CAN BE DONE?

1. Who by unending discipline of the senses embraces unity cannot be disin-

tegrated. By concentrating his vitality and inducing tenderness he can become like a little child. By purifying, by cleansing and profound intuition he can be free from faults.

2. Who loves the people when administering the country will practise non-assertion.

Opening and closing the gates of heaven, he will be like a mother-bird; bright, and white, and penetrating the four quarters, he will be unsophisticated. He quickens them and feeds them. He quickens but owns not. He acts but claims not. He excels but rules not. This is called profound virtue.

11. THE FUNCTION OF THE NON-EXISTENT.

1. Thirty spokes unite in one nave and on that which is non-existent [on the hole in the nave] depends the wheel's utility. Clay is moulded into a vessel and on that which is non-existent [on its hollowness] depends the vessel's utility. By cutting out doors and windows we build a house and on that which is

non-existent [on the empty space within]
depends the house's utility.

2. Therefore, existence renders actual
but non-existence renders useful.

12. ABSTAINING FROM DESIRE.

1. "The five colors [combined] the hu-
    man eye will blind;
    The five notes [in one sound] the hu-
    man ear confound;
    The five tastes [when they blend] the
    human mouth offend."
2. "Racing and hunting will human
    hearts turn mad,
    Treasures high-prized make human
    conduct bad."
3. Therefore
The holy man attends to the inner and
not to the outer. He abandons the latter
and chooses the former.

13. LOATHING SHAME.

1. "Favor bodes disgrace; it is like trem-
    bling.
    Rank bodes great heartache. It is
    like the body."

2. What means "Favor bodes disgrace; it is like trembling?"

Favor humiliates. Its acquisition causes trembling, its loss causes trembling. This is meant by "Favor bodes disgrace; it is like trembling."

3. What means "Rank bodes great heartache, it is like the body?"

I suffer great heartache because I have a body. When I have no body, what heartache remains?

4. Therefore who administers the empire as he takes care of his body can be entrusted with the empire.

14. PRAISING THE MYSTERIOUS.

1. We look at Reason and do not see it; its name is Colorless. We listen to Reason and do not hear it; its name is Soundless. We grope for Reason and do not grasp it; its name is Bodiless.

2. These three things cannot further be analyzed. Thus they are combined and conceived as a unity which on its surface is not clear and in its depth not obscure.

3. Forever and aye Reason remains un-

namable, and again and again it returns home to non-existence.

4. This is called the form of the formless, the image of the imageless. This is called the transcendentally abstruse.

5. In front its beginning is not seen. In the rear its end is not seen.

6. By holding fast to the Reason of the ancients, the present is mastered and the origin of the past understood. This is called Reason's clue.

15. THE REVEALERS OF VIRTUE.

1. Those of yore who have succeeded in becoming masters are subtile, spiritual, profound, and penetrating. On account of their profundity they can not be understood. Because they can not be understood, therefore I endeavor to make them intelligible.

2. How cautious they are! Like men in winter crossing a river. How reluctant! Like men fearing in the four quarters their neighbors. How reserved! They behave like guests. How elusive! They resemble ice when melting. How simple! They resemble rough wood.

How empty! They resemble the valley.
How obscure! They resemble troubled
waters.

3. Who by quieting can gradually render muddy waters clear? Who by stirring can gradually quicken the still?

4. He who cherishes this Reason is
not anxious to be filled. Since he is not
filled, therefore he may grow old; without renewal he is complete.

16. RETURNING TO THE ROOT.

1. By attaining the height of abstraction we gain fulness of rest.

2. All the ten thousand things arise,
and I see them return. Now they bloom
in bloom but each one homeward returneth to its root.

3. Returning to the root means rest.
It signifies the return according to destiny. Return according to destiny means
the eternal. Knowing the eternal means
enlightenment. Not knowing the eternal causes passions to rise; and that is
evil.

4. Knowing the eternal renders comprehensive. Comprehensiveness renders

broad. Breadth renders royal. Royalty renders heavenly. Heaven renders Reason-like. Reason renders lasting. Thus the decay of the body implies no danger.

17. SIMPLICITY IN HABITS.

1. Of great rulers the subjects do not notice the existence. To lesser ones people are attached; they praise them. Still lesser ones people fear, and the meanest ones people despise.

2. For it is said:

"If your faith be insufficient, verily, you will receive no faith."

3. How reluctantly they [the great rulers] considered their words! Merit they accomplished; deeds they performed; and the hundred families thought: "We are independent."

18. THE PALLIATION OF VULGARITY.

1. When the great Reason is obliterated, we have benevolence and justice. Prudence and circumspection appear, and we have much hypocrisy.

2. When family relations no longer harmonize, we have filial piety and pa-

ternal devotion. When the country and
the clans decay through disorder, we
have loyalty and allegiance.

19. RETURNING TO SIMPLICITY.

1. Abandon your saintliness; put away
your prudence; and the people will gain
a hundredfold!

2. Abandon your benevolence; put
away your justice; and the people will
return to filial piety and paternal devotion.

3. Abandon smartness; give up greed;
and thieves and robbers will no longer
exist.

4. These are three things for which
culture is insufficient. Therefore it is
said:

"Hold fast to that which will endure,
    Show thyself simple, preserve thee
        pure,
And lessen self with desires fewer."

20. DIFFERENT FROM THE VULGAR.

1. Abandon learnedness, and you have
no vexation. The "yes" compared with
the "yea," how little do they differ!

But the good compared with the bad, how much do they differ!

2. If what the people dread cannot be made dreadless, there will be desolation, alas! and verily, there will be no end of it.

3. The multitudes of men are happy, so happy, as though celebrating a great feast. They are as though in springtime ascending a tower. I alone remain quiet, alas! like one that has not yet received an omen. I am like unto a babe that does not yet smile.

4. Forlorn am I, O so forlorn! It appears that I have no place whither I may return home.

5. The multitude of men all have plenty and I alone appear empty. Alas! I am a man whose heart is foolish.

6. Ignorant am I, O, so ignorant! Common people are bright, so bright, I alone am dull.

7. Common people are smart, so smart, I alone am confused, so confused.

8. Desolate am I, alas! like the sea. Adrift, alas! like one who has no place where to stay.

9. The multitude of men all possess usefulness. I alone am awkward and a rustic too. I alone differ from others, but I prize seeking sustenance from our mother.

21. EMPTYING THE HEART.

1. "Vast virtue's form
   Follows Reason's norm.

2. "And Reason's nature
   Is vague and eluding.

3. "How eluding and vague
   All types including!
   How vague and eluding,
   All beings including!
   How deep and how obscure.
   It harbors the spirit pure,
   Whose truth is ever sure,
   Whose faith abides for aye
   From of yore until to-day.

4. "Its name is never vanishing,
   It heeds the good of everything."

5. Through what do I know that "it heeds the good of everything"? In this way, verily: Through IT.

22. HUMILITY'S INCREASE.

1. "The crooked shall be straight,
    Crushed ones recuperate,
    The empty find their fill.
    The worn with strength shall thrill;
    Who little have receive,
    And who have much will grieve."

2. Therefore
The holy man embraces unity and becomes for all the world a model.
    Not self-displaying he is enlightened;
    Not self-approving he is distinguished;
    Not self-asserting he acquires merit;
    Not self-seeking he gaineth life.
    Since he does not quarrel, therefore no one in the world can quarrel with him.

3. The saying of the ancients: "The crooked shall be straight," is it in any way vainly spoken? Verily, they will be straightened and return home.

23. EMPTINESS AND NON-EXISTENCE.

1. To be taciturn is the natural way. A hurricane does not outlast the morn-

ing.   A cloudburst does not outlast the
day.

2. Who causes these events but heaven
and earth?   If even heaven and earth
cannot be unremitting, will not man be
much less so?

3. Those who pursue their business in
Reason, men of Reason, associate in Reason.   Those who pursue their business
in virtue associate in virtue.   Those who
pursue their business in ill luck associate in ill luck.   When men associate
in Reason, Reason makes them glad to
find companions.   When men associate
in virtue, virtue makes them glad to
find companions.   When men associate
in ill luck, ill luck makes them glad to
find companions.

"If your faith is insufficient, verily
shall ye receive no faith."

24. TROUBLE FROM INDULGENCE.

1. One on tiptoe is not steady;
   One astride makes no advance.
   Self-displayers are not enlightened,
   Self-asserters lack distinction,

Self-approvers have no merit,
And self-seekers stunt their lives.

2. Before Reason this is like surfeit
of food; it is like a wen on the body
with which people are apt to be disgusted.

3. Therefore the man of reason will
not indulge in it.

25. IMAGING THE MYSTERIOUS.

1. There is a Being wondrous and complete. Before heaven and earth, it was.
How calm it is! How spiritual!

2. Alone it standeth, and it changeth
not; around it moveth, and it suffereth
not; yet therefore can it be the world's
mother.

3. Its name I know not, but its nature
I call Reason.

4. Constrained to give a name, I call
it the great. The great I call the departing, and the departing I call the
beyond. The beyond I call home.

5. The saying goes: "Reason is great,
heaven is great, earth is great, and royalty also is great. [There are four things

in the world that are great, and royalty is one of them.]

6. Man's standard is the earth. The earth's standard is heaven. Heaven's standard is Reason. Reason's standard is intrinsic.

26. THE VIRTUE OF GRAVITY.

1. The heavy is of the light the root, and rest is motion's master.

2. Therefore the holy man in his daily walk does not depart from gravity. Although he may have magnificent sights, he calmly sits with liberated mind.

3. But how is it when the master of the ten thousand chariots in his personal conduct is too light for the empire? If he is too light he will lose his vassals. If he is too passionate he will lose the throne.

27. THE FUNCTION OF SKILL.

1. "Good travelers leave no trace nor track,
Good speakers, in logic show no lack,
Good counters need no counting rack.

2. "Good lockers bolting bars need not,
    Yet none their locks can loose.
   Good binders need no string nor knot,
    Yet none unties their noose."

3. Therefore the holy man is always a good saviour of men, for there are no outcast people. He is always a good saviour of things, for there are no outcast things. This is called applied enlightenment.

4. Thus the good man does not respect multitudes of men. The bad man respects the people's wealth. Who does not esteem multitudes nor is charmed by their wealth, though his knowledge be greatly confused, he must be recognized as profoundly spiritual.

28. RETURNING TO SIMPLICITY.

1. "Who his manhood shows
   And his womanhood knows
   Becomes the empire's river.
   Is he the empire's river,
   He will from virtue never deviate,
   And home he turneth to a child's estate.

2. "Who his brightness shows
   And his blackness knows
   Becomes the empire's model.
   Is he the empire's model,
   Of virtue ne'er shall he be destitute,
   And home he turneth to the absolute.

3. "Who knows his fame
   And guards his shame
   Becomes the empire's valley.
   Is he the empire's valley,
   For e'er his virtue will sufficient be,
   And home he turneth to simplicity."

4. Simplicity, when scattered, becomes a vessel of usefulness. The holy man, by using it, becomes the chief leader; and truly, a great principle will never do harm.

29. NON-ASSERTION.

1. When one desires to take in hand the empire and make it, I see him not succeed. The empire is a divine vessel which cannot be made. One who makes it, mars it. One who takes it, loses it.

2. And it is said of beings:
"Some are obsequious, others move
  boldly,
Some breathe warmly, others coldly,
Some are strong and others weak,
Some rise proudly, others sneak."

3. Therefore the holy man abandons excess, he abandons extravagance, he abandons indulgence.

30. BE CHARY OF WAR.

1. He who with Reason assists the master of mankind will not with arms strengthen the empire. His methods invite requital.

2. Where armies are quartered briars and thorns grow. Great wars unfailingly are followed by famines. A good man acts resolutely and then stops. He ventures not to take by force.

3. Be resolute but not boastful; resolute but not haughty; resolute but not arrogant; resolute because you cannot avoid it; resolute but not violent.

4. Things thrive and then grow old.

This is called un-Reason. Un-Reason
soon ceases.

31. QUELLING WAR.

1. Even victorious arms are unblest
among tools, and people had better shun
them.   Therefore he who has Reason
does not rely on them.

2. The superior man when residing at
home honors the left. When using arms,
he honors the right.

3. Arms are unblest among tools and
not the superior man's tools. Only when
it is unavoidable he uses them. Peace
and quietude he holdeth high.

4. He conquers but rejoices not. Re-
joicing at a conquest means to enjoy
the slaughter of men. He who enjoys
the slaughter of men will most assuredly
not obtain his will in the empire.

32. THE VIRTUE OF HOLINESS.

1. Reason, in its eternal aspect, is unnamable.

2. Although its simplicity seems insignificant, the whole world does not
dare to suppress it. If princes and kings

could keep it, the ten thousand things would of themselves pay homage. Heaven and earth would unite in dripping sweet dew, and the people with no one to command them would of themselves be righteous.

3. As soon as Reason creates order, it becomes namable. Whenever the namable in its turn acquires existence, one learns to know when to stop. By knowing when to stop, one avoids danger.

4. To illustrate Reason's relation to the world we compare it to streams and creeks in their course towards rivers and the ocean.

33. THE VIRTUE OF DISCRIMINATION.

1. One who knows others is clever, but one who knows himself is enlightened.

2. One who conquers others is powerful, but one who conquers himself is mighty.

3. One who knows contentment is rich and one who pushes with vigor has will.

4. One who loses not his place endures.

5. One who may die but will not perish, has life everlasting.

34. TRUST IN ITS PERFECTION.

1. How all-pervading is the great Reason! It can be on the left and it can be on the right.

2. The ten thousand things depend upon it for their life, and it refuses them not. When its merit is accomplished it assumes not the name. Lovingly it nourishes the ten thousand things and plays not the lord. Ever desireless it can be classed with the small. The ten thousand things return home to it. It plays not the lord. It can be classed with the great.

3. Therefore
The holy man unto death does not make himself great and can thus accomplish his greatness.

35. THE VIRTUE OF BENEVOLENCE.

1. "Who holdeth fast to the great Form,
Of him the world will come in quest:
For there we never meet with harm,
There we find shelter, comfort, rest."

2. Music with dainties makes the passing stranger stop. But Reason, when

coming from the mouth, how tasteless is it! It has no flavor. When looked at, there is not enough to be seen; when listened to, there is not enough to be heard. However, when used, it is inexhaustible.

36. THE SECRET'S EXPLANATION.

1. That which is about to contract has surely been expanded. That which is about to weaken has surely been strengthened. That which is about to fall has surely been raised. That which is about to be despoiled has surely been endowed.

2. This is an explanation of the secret that the tender and the weak conquer the hard and the strong.

3. As the fish should not escape from the deep, so with the country's sharp tools the people should not become acquainted.

37. ADMINISTRATION OF GOVERNMENT.

1. Reason always practises non-assertion, and there is nothing that remains undone.

2. If princes and kings could keep Reason, the ten thousand creatures would of themselves be reformed. While being reformed they might yet be anxious to stir; but I would restrain them by the simplicity of the Ineffable.

3. "The simplicity of the unexpressed
Will purify the heart of lust.
Is there no lust there will be rest,
And all the world will thus be blest."

II.
38. DISCOURSE ON VIRTUE.

1. Superior virtue is unvirtue. Therefore it has virtue. Inferior virtue never loses sight of virtue. Therefore it has no virtue.

2. Superior virtue is non-assertion and without pretension. Inferior virtue asserts and makes pretensions.

3. Superior benevolence acts but makes no pretensions. Superior justice acts and makes pretensions.

4. Superior propriety acts and when

no one responds to it, it stretches its arm and enforces its rules.

5. Thus one loses Reason and then virtue appears. One loses virtue and then benevolence appears. One loses benevolence and then justice appears. One loses justice and then propriety appears. The rules of propriety are the semblance of loyalty and faith, and the beginning of disorder.

6. Traditionalism is the flower of Reason, but of ignorance the beginning.

7. Therefore a great organizer abides by the solid and dwells not in the external. He abides in the fruit and dwells not in the flower.

8. Therefore he discards the latter and chooses the former.

39. THE ROOT OF ORDER.

1. From of old these things have obtained oneness:

2. "Heaven by oneness becometh pure.
Earth by oneness can endure.
Minds by oneness souls procure.
Valleys by oneness repletion secure.

"All creatures by oneness to life have
been called.
And kings were by oneness as models
installed."

Such is the result of oneness.

3. "Were heaven not pure it might be
rent.
Were earth not stable it might be
bent.
Were minds not ensouled they'd be
impotent.
Were valleys not filled they'd soon
be spent.
When creatures are lifeless who can
their death prevent?
Are kings not models, but on haughti-
ness bent,
Their fall, forsooth, is imminent."

4. Thus, the nobles come from the com-
moners as their root, and the high rest
upon the lowly as their foundation.
Therefore, princes and kings call themselves orphaned, lonely, and unworthy.
Is this not because they take lowliness
as their root?

5. The several parts of a carriage are not a carriage.

6. Those who have become a unity are neither anxious to be praised with praise like a gem, nor disdained with disdain like a stone.

40. AVOIDING ACTIVITY.

1. "Homeward is Reason's course,
   Weakness is Reason's force."

2. Heaven and earth and the ten thousand things come from existence, but existence comes from non-existence.

41. SAMENESS IN DIFFERENCE.

1. When a superior scholar hears of Reason he endeavors to practise it.

2. When an average scholar hears of Reason he will sometimes keep it and sometimes lose it.

3. When an inferior scholar hears of Reason he will greatly ridicule it. Were it not thus ridiculed, it would as Reason be insufficient.

4. Therefore the poet says:

5. "The Reason-enlightened seem dark and black,

The Reason - advanced seem going
back,
The Reason - straight - levelled seem
rugged and slack.

6. "The high in virtue resemble a vale,
The purely white in shame must
quail,
The staunchest virtue seems to fail.

7. "The solidest virtue seems not alert,
The purest chastity seems pervert,
The greatest square will rightness
desert.

8. "The largest vessel is not yet complete,
The loudest sound is not speech re-
plete,
The greatest form has no shape concrete."

9. Reason so long as it remains latent
is unnamable. Yet Reason alone is good
for imparting and completing.

42. REASON'S MODIFICATIONS.

1. Reason begets unity; unity begets
duality; duality begets trinity; and trinity begets the ten thousand things.

2. The ten thousand things are sustained by Yin [the negative principle]; they are encompassed by Yang [the positive principle], and the immaterial breath renders them harmonious.

3. That which the people find odious, to be orphaned, lonely, and unworthy, kings and princes select as their titles. Thus, on the one hand, loss implies gain, and on the other hand, gain implies loss.

4. What others have taught I teach also.

5. The strong and aggressive do not die a natural death; but I will obey the doctrine's father.

43. ITS UNIVERSAL APPLICATION.

1. The world's weakest overcomes the world's hardest.

2. Non-existence enters into the impenetrable.

3. Thereby I comprehend of non-assertion the advantage. There are few in the world who obtain of non-assertion the advantage and of silence the lesson.

44. SETTING UP PRECEPTS.

1. "Name or person, which is more near?
   Person or fortune, which is more dear?
   Gain or loss, which is more sear?

2. "Extreme dotage leadeth to squandering.
   Hoarded wealth inviteth plundering.

3. "Who is content incurs no humiliation,
   Who knows when to stop risks no vitiation,
   Forever lasteth his duration."

45. GREATEST VIRTUE.

1. "Greatest perfection imperfect will be,
   But its work ne'er waneth.
   Greatest fulness is vacuity,
   Its work unexhausted remaineth."

2. "Straightest lines resemble curves;
   Greatest skill like a tyro serves;
   Greatest eloquence stammers and swerves."

3. Motion conquers cold.   Quietude

conquers heat.   Purity and clearness are the world's standard.

46. MODERATION OF DESIRE.

1. When the world possesses Reason, race horses are reserved for hauling dung. When the world is without Reason, war horses are bred in the common.

2. No greater sin than yielding to desire.   No greater misery than discontent.   No greater calamity than greed.

3. Therefore, he who knows content's content is always content.

47. VIEWING THE DISTANT.

1. "Without passing out of the gate
  The world's course I prognosticate.
  Without peeping through the window
  The heavenly Reason I contemplate.
  The further one goes,
  The less one knows."

2. Therefore the holy man does not travel, and yet he has knowledge. He does not see things, and yet he defines them. He does not labor, and yet he completes.

48. FORGETTING KNOWLEDGE.

1. He who seeks learnedness will daily increase. He who seeks Reason will daily diminish. He will diminish and continue to diminish until he arrives at non-assertion.

2. With non-assertion there is nothing that he cannot achieve. When he takes the empire, it is always because he uses no diplomacy. He who uses diplomacy is not fit to take the empire.

49. TRUST IN VIRTUE.

1. The holy man has not a heart of his own. The hundred families' hearts he makes his heart.

2. The good I meet with goodness; the bad I also meet with goodness; that is virtue's goodness. The faithful I meet with faith; the faithless I also meet with faith; that is virtue's faith.

3. The holy man dwells in the world anxious, very anxious in his dealings with the world. He universalizes his heart, and the hundred families fix upon

him their ears and eyes. The holy man
treats them all like children.

50. THE ESTIMATION OF LIFE.

1. Abroad in life, home in death.

2. There are thirteen avenues of life;
there are thirteen avenues of death; on
thirteen avenues men that live pass unto
the realm of death.

3. Now, what is the reason? It is because they live life's intensity.

4. Yea, I understand that one whose
life is based on goodness, when traveling
on land will not fall a prey to the rhinoceros or the tiger. When coming
among soldiers, he need not fear arms
and weapons. The rhinoceros finds no
place wherein to insert its horn. The
tiger finds no place wherein to put his
claws. Weapons find no place wherein to
thrust their blades. The reason is that
he does not belong to the realm of death.

51. NURSING VIRTUE.

1. Reason quickens all creatures. Virtue feeds them. Reality shapes them.
The forces complete them. Therefore

among the ten thousand things there is none that does not esteem Reason and honor virtue.

2. Since the esteem of Reason and the honoring of virtue is by no one commanded, it is forever spontaneous.

3. Therefore it is said that Reason quickens all creatures, while virtue feeds them, raises them, nurtures them, completes them, matures them, rears them, and protects them.

4. To quicken but not to own, to make but not to claim, to raise but not to rule, this is called profound virtue.

52. RETURNING TO THE ORIGIN.

1. When the world takes its beginning, Reason becomes the world's mother.

2. As one knows his mother, so she in turn knows her child; as she quickens her child, so he in turn keeps to his mother, and to the end of life he is not in danger. Who closes his mouth, and shuts his sense-gates, in the end of life he will encounter no trouble; but who opens his mouth and meddles with af-

fairs, in the end of life he cannot be saved.

3. Who beholds his smallness is called enlightened. Who preserves his tenderness is called strong. Who uses Reason's light and returns home to its enlightenment does not surrender his person to perdition. This is called practising the eternal.

53. GAINING INSIGHT.

1. If I have ever so little knowledge, I shall walk in the great Reason. It is but expansion that I must fear.

2. The great Reason is very plain, but people are fond of by-paths.

3. When the palace is very splendid, the fields are very weedy and granaries very empty.

4. To wear ornaments and gay clothes, to carry sharp swords, to be excessive in drinking and eating, to have a redundance of costly articles, this is the pride of robbers.

5. Surely, this is un-Reason.

54. THE CULTIVATION OF INTUITION.

1. "What is well planted is not uprooted;
   What's well preserved can not be
      looted!"

2. By sons and grandsons the sacrificial celebrations shall not cease.

3. Who cultivates Reason in his person, his virtue is genuine.

Who cultivates it in his house, his virtue is overflowing.

Who cultivates it in his township, his virtue is lasting.

Who cultivates it in his country, his virtue is abundant.

Who cultivates it in the world, his virtue is universal.

4. Therefore,

By one's person one tests persons.

By one's house one tests houses.

By one's township one tests townships.

By one's country one tests countries.

By one's world one tests worlds.

5. How do I know that the world is such? Through IT.

55. THE SIGNET OF THE MYSTERIOUS.

1. He who possesses virtue in all its solidity is like unto a little child.

2. Venomous reptiles do not sting him, fierce beasts do not seize him. Birds of prey do not strike him. His bones are weak, his sinews tender, but his grasp is firm. He does not yet know the relation between male and female, but his virility is strong. Thus his metal grows to perfection. A whole day he might cry and sob without growing hoarse. This shows the perfection of his harmony.

3. To know the harmonious is called the eternal. To know the eternal is called enlightenment.

4. To increase life is called a blessing, and heart - directed vitality is called strength, but things vigorous are about to grow old and I call this un-Reason.

5. Un-Reason soon ceases!

56. THE VIRTUE OF THE MYSTERIOUS.

1. One who knows does not talk. One who talks does not know. Therefore the sage keeps his mouth shut and his sense-gates closed.

2. "He will blunt his own sharpness,
His own tangles adjust;
He will dim his own radiance,
And be one with his dust."

3. This is called profound identification.

4. Thus he is inaccessible to love and also inaccessible to enmity. He is inaccessible to profit and inaccessible to loss. He is also inaccessible to favor and inaccessible to disgrace. Thus he becomes world-honored.

57. SIMPLICITY IN HABITS.

1. With rectitude one governs the state; with craftiness one leads the army; with non-diplomacy one takes the empire. How do I know that it is so? Through IT.

2. The more restrictions and prohibitions are in the empire, the poorer grow the people. The more weapons the people have, the more troubled is the state. The more there is cunning and skill, the more startling events will happen. The

more mandates and laws are enacted, the more there will be thieves and robbers.

3. Therefore the holy man says: I practise non-assertion, and the people of themselves reform. I love quietude, and the people of themselves become righteous. I use no diplomacy, and the people of themselves become rich. I have no desire, and the people of themselves remain simple.

58. ADAPTATION TO CHANGE.

1. Whose government is unostentatious, quite unostentatious, his people will be prosperous, quite prosperous. Whose government is prying, quite prying, his people will be needy, quite needy.

2. Misery, alas! rests upon happiness. Happiness, alas! underlies misery. But who foresees the catastrophe? It will not be prevented!

3. What is ordinary becomes again extraordinary. What is good becomes again unpropitious. This bewilders people, and it happens constantly since times immemorial.

4. Therefore the holy man is square but not sharp, strict but not obnoxious, upright but not restraining, bright but not dazzling.

59. HOLD FAST TO REASON.

1. To govern the people is the affair of heaven and there is nothing like thrift.

Now consider that thrift is said to come from early practice.

2. By early practice it is said that we can accumulate an abundance of virtue. If one accumulates an abundance of virtue then there is nothing that can not be overcome.

3. When nothing can not be overcome then no one knows his limit. When no one knows his limit one can have possession of the commonwealth.

4. Who has possession of the commonwealth's mother [thrift] may last and abide.

5. This is called the possession of deep roots and of a staunch stem. To life, to everlastingness, to comprehension, this is the way.

60. HOW TO MAINTAIN ONE'S PLACE.

1. Govern a great country as you would fry small fish: [neither gut nor scale them.]

2. If with Reason the empire is managed, its ghosts will not spook. Not only will its ghosts not spook, but its gods will not harm the people. Not only will its gods not harm the people, but neither will its holy men harm the people. Since neither will do harm, therefore their virtues will be combined.

61. THE VIRTUE OF HUMILITY.

1. A great state, one that lowly flows, becomes the empire's union, and the empire's wife.

2. The wife always through quietude conquers her husband, and by quietude renders herself lowly.

3. Thus a great state through lowliness toward small states will conquer the small states, and small states through lowliness toward great states will conquer great states.

4. Therefore some render themselves

lowly for the purpose of conquering; others are lowly and therefore conquer.

5. A great state desires no more than to unite and feed the people; a small state desires no more than to devote itself to the service of the people; but that both may obtain their wishes, the greater one must stoop.

62. PRACTISE REASON.

1. The man of Reason is the ten thousand creatures' refuge, the good man's wealth, the bad man's stay.

2. With beautiful words one can sell. With honest conduct one can do still more with the people.

3. If a man be bad, why should he be thrown away? Therefore, an emperor was elected and three ministers appointed; but better than holding before one's face the jade table [of the ministry] and riding with four horses, is sitting still and propounding the eternal Reason.

4. Why do the ancients prize this Reason? Is it not, say, because when sought

it is obtained and the sinner thereby can be saved?   Therefore it is world-honored.

63. CONSIDER BEGINNINGS.

1. Assert non-assertion.
Practise non-practice.
Taste the tasteless.
Make great the small.
Make much the little.
2. Requite hatred with virtue.
3. Contemplate a difficulty when it is easy.   Manage a great thing when it is small.
4. The world's most difficult undertakings necessarily originate while easy, and the world's greatest undertakings necessarily originate while small.
5. Therefore the holy man to the end does not venture to play the great, and thus he can accomplish his greatness.
6. Rash promises surely lack faith, and many easy things surely involve in many difficulties.
7. Therefore, the holy man regards everything as difficult, and thus to the end encounters no difficulties.

64. MIND THE INSIGNIFICANT.

1. What is still at rest is easily kept quiet. What has not as yet appeared is easily prevented. What is still feeble is easily broken. What is still scant is easily dispersed.

2. Treat things before they exist. Regulate things before disorder begins. The stout tree has originated from a tiny rootlet. A tower of nine stories is raised by heaping up [bricks of] clay. A thousand miles' journey begins with a foot.

3. He that makes mars. He that grasps loses.

The holy man does not make; therefore he mars not. He does not grasp; therefore he loses not. The people when undertaking an enterprise are always near completion, and yet they fail.

4. Remain careful to the end as in the beginning and you will not fail in your enterprise.

5. Therefore the holy man desires to be desireless, and does not prize articles difficult to obtain. He learns, not to

be learned, and seeks a home where multitudes of people pass by.

6. He assists the ten thousand things in their natural development, but he does not venture to interfere.

65. THE VIRTUE OF SIMPLICITY.

1. The ancients who were well versed in Reason did not thereby enlighten the people; they intended thereby to make them simple-hearted.

2. If people are difficult to govern, it is because they are too smart. To govern the country with smartness is the country's curse. To govern the country without smartness is the country's blessing. He who knows these two things is also a model [like the ancients]. Always to know the model is called profound virtue.

3. Spiritual virtue, verily, is profound. Verily, it is far-reaching. Verily, it is to everything reverse. But then it will procure great recognition.

66. PUTTING ONESELF BEHIND.

1. That rivers and oceans can of the hundred valleys be kings is due to their excelling in lowliness. Thus they can of the hundred valleys be the kings.

2. Therefore the holy man, when anxious to be above the people, must in his words keep underneath them. When anxious to lead the people, he must with his person keep behind them.

3. Therefore the holy man dwells above, but the people are not burdened. He is ahead, but the people suffer no harm.

4. Therefore the world rejoices in exalting him and does not tire. Because he strives not, no one in the world will strive with him.

67. THE THREE TREASURES.

1. All in the world call me great; but I resemble the unlikely. Now a man is great only because he resembles the unlikely. Did he resemble the likely, how lasting, indeed, would his mediocrity be!

2. I have three treasures which I

cherish and prize. The first is called compassion. The second is called economy. The third is called not daring to come to the front in the world.

3. The compassionate can be brave; the economical can be generous; those who dare not come to the front in the world can become perfect as chief vessels.

4. Now, if people discard compassion and are brave; if they discard economy and are generous; if they discard modesty and are ambitious, they will surely die.

5. Now, the compassionate will in attack be victorious, and in defence firm. Heaven when about to save one will with compassion protect him.

68. COMPLYING WITH HEAVEN.

1. He who excels as a warrior is not warlike. He who excels as a fighter is not wrathful. He who excels in conquering the enemy does not strive. He who excels in employing men is lowly.

2. This is called the virtue of not-striving. This is called utilizing men's

ability. This is called complying with
heaven—since olden times the highest.

69. THE FUNCTION OF THE MYSTE-RIOUS.

1. A military expert used to say: "I
dare not act as host [who takes the ini-
tiative] but act as guest [with reserve].
I dare not advance an inch, but I withdraw a foot."

2. This is called marching without
marching, threatening without arms,
charging without hostility, seizing without weapons.

3. No greater misfortune than making
light of the enemy! When we make
light of the enemy, it is almost as though
we had lost our treasure—[compassion].

4. Thus, if matched armies encounter
one another, the one who does so in sor-
row is sure to conquer.

70. DIFFICULT TO UNDERSTAND.

1. My words are very easy to understand and very easy to practise, but in
the world no one can understand, no one
can practise them.

2. Words have an ancestor; Deeds have a master [viz., Reason]. Since he is not understood, therefore I am not understood. Those who understand me are few, and thus I am distinguished.

3. Therefore the holy man wears wool, and hides in his bosom his jewels.

71. THE DISEASE OF KNOWLEDGE.

1. To know the unknowable, that is elevating. Not to know the knowable, that is sickness.

2. Only by becoming sick of sickness can we be without sickness.

3. The holy man is not sick. Because he is sick of sickness, therefore he is not sick.

72. HOLDING ONESELF DEAR.

1. If the people do not fear the dreadful, the great dreadful will come, surely.

2. Let them not deem their lives narrow. Let them not deem their lot wearisome. When it is not deemed wearisome, then it will not be wearisome.

3. Therefore the holy man knows himself but does not display himself. He

holds himself dear but does not honor himself. Thus he discards the latter and chooses the former.

73. DARING TO ACT.

1. Courage, if carried to daring, leads to death; courage, if not carried to daring, leads to life. Either of these two things is sometimes beneficial, sometimes harmful.

2. "Why 't is by heaven rejected,
Who has the reason detected?"

Therefore the holy man also regards it as difficult.

3. The Heavenly Reason strives not, but it is sure to conquer. It speaks not, but it is sure to respond. It summons not, but it comes of itself. It works patiently, but is sure in its designs.

4. Heaven's net is vast, so vast. It is wide-meshed, but it loses nothing.

74. OVERCOME DELUSION.

1. If the people do not fear death, how can they be frightened by death? If we make people fear death, and sup-

posing some would [still] venture to rebel, if we seize them for capital punishment, who will dare?

2. There is always an executioner who kills. Now to take the place of the executioner who kills is taking the place of the great carpenter who hews. If a man takes the place of the great carpenter who hews, he will rarely, indeed, fail to injure his hand.

75. HARMED THROUGH GREED.

1. The people hunger because their superiors consume too many taxes; therefore they hunger. The people are difficult to govern because their superiors are too meddlesome; therefore they are difficult to govern. The people make light of death on account of the intensity of their clinging to life; therefore they make light of death.

2. He who is not bent on life is worthier than he who esteems life.

76. BEWARE OF STRENGTH.

1. Man during life is tender and delicate. When he dies he is stiff and stark.

2. The ten thousand things, the grass as well as the trees, while they live are tender and supple. When they die they are rigid and dry.

3. Thus the hard and the strong are the companions of death. The tender and the delicate are the companions of life.

Therefore he who in arms is strong will not conquer.

4. When a tree has grown strong it is doomed.

5. The strong and the great stay below. The tender and the delicate stay above.

77. HEAVEN'S REASON.

1. Is not Heaven's Reason truly like stretching a bow? The high it brings down, the lowly it lifts up. Those who have abundance it depleteth; those who are deficient it augmenteth.

2. Such is Heaven's Reason. It depleteth those who have abundance but completeth the deficient.

3. Man's Reason is not so. He depleteth the deficient in order to serve those who have abundance.

4. Where is he who would have abundance for serving the world?

5. Indeed, it is the holy man who acts but claims not; merit he acquires but he does not dwell upon it, and does he ever show any anxiety to display his excellence?

78. TRUST IN FAITH.

1. In the world nothing is tenderer and more delicate than water. In attacking the hard and the strong nothing will surpass it. There is nothing that herein takes its place.

2. The weak conquer the strong, the tender conquer the rigid. In the world there is no one who does not know it, but no one will practise it.

3. Therefore the holy man says:

"Him who the country's sin makes his,
We hail as priest at the great sacrifice.
Him who the curse bears of the country's failing.
As king of the empire we are hailing."

4. True words seem paradoxical.

79. KEEP YOUR OBLIGATIONS.

1. When a great hatred is reconciled, naturally some hatred will remain. How can this be made good?

2. Therefore the sage keeps the obligations of his contract and exacts not from others. Those who have virtue attend to their obligations; those who have no virtue attend to their claims.

3. Heaven's Reason shows no preference but always assists the good man.

80. REMAINING IN ISOLATION.

1. In a small country with few people let there be aldermen and mayors who are possessed of power over men but would not use it. Induce people to grieve at death but do not cause them to move to a distance. Although they had ships and carriages, they should find no occasion to ride in them. Although they had armours and weapons, they should find no occasion to don them.

2 Induce people to return to [the old custom of] knotted cords and to use them [in the place of writing], to de-

light in their food, to be proud of their clothes, to be content with their homes, and to rejoice in their customs: then in a neighboring state within sight, the voices of the cocks and dogs would be within hearing, yet the people might grow old and die before they visited one another.

81. PROPOUNDING THE ESSENTIAL.

1. True words are not pleasant; pleasant words are not true. The good are not contentious; the contentious are not good. The wise are not learned; the learned are not wise.

2. The holy man hoards not. The more he does for others, the more he owns himself. The more he gives to others, the more will he himself lay up an abundance.

3. Heaven's Reason is to benefit but not to injure; the holy man's Reason is to accomplish but not to strive.

COMMENTS AND ALTERNATIVE READINGS.

CHAPTER 1.

The phrase '*yiu ming*, "having name" (or simply *ming*, "name") means that which the definition of a name involves, and as such the term represents the actualized types of things. However *wu ming*, "not name" or "the Unnamable," corresponds to Plato's conception of the prototype of things before they have been actualized. Lao-tze speaks with reverence of the Unnamable,[1] which closely corresponds to the "Ineffable" of Western mystics.

The words "these two things" apparently refer to the Unnamable and the Namable.

What Lao-tze calls "the Name" or "the

[1] See also Chapters 32 and 41.

Namable" is in Spinoza's language *natura naturata,* while "the Unnamable" is *natura naturans.* In either system the two are one; they are two aspects of one and the same thing which in Laotze's taoism is the Tao and in Spinoza's cosmotheism is God as the eternal substance.

CHAPTER 2.

The first sentence reads literally, "Under the heavens [*i. e.,* all over the world, or everywhere] all know [i. e., it is obvious], if beauty acts beauty it is only ugliness." The verb "acts" is to be taken in the same sense as it is used in English, viz., "making a display or show of."

We deem our present rendering an improvement on our former version.

According to a notion of the early Christians the devil would like to play the part of God, as Tertullian says, *Satanas affectat sacramenta Dei.* On Lao-tze's theory the nature of the devil consists exactly in the attempt of acting the part of God.

The close interrelation of goodness
with badness and of beauty with ugliness suggests the quotation on oppo-
sites. It sets forth the coexistence of
contrasts, and their mutual dependence
is more obvious to the Chinese than to
other nations, because in their word-
combinations they use compounds of
contrasts to denote what is common in
both. Thus a combination of the words
"to be" and "not to be" means the strug-
gle for life, or the bread question; "the
high and the low" means altitude;
"much and little" means quantity, etc.
But what originally seems to have been
the trivial observation of a grammar-
school teacher acquires a philosophical
meaning when commented upon by Lao-
tze.

CHAPTER 3.

In former editions we have translated
the verb *shang* by its common meaning
"to exalt," but here it is obviously a re-
flex verb meaning "to exalt oneself" or
"to brag, to boast."

The word *fu* means literally "stomach"

or "the interior," but it may also mean "soul," for according to Chinese ideas the soul has its seat in the stomach.

The idea that the belly is the noblest part of the body where tender sentiments dwell was quite common among early peoples. Thus, e. g. the Hebrew *rakhamim*,[2] which originally means "entrails," is used in the sense of "compassion" and "love." In Japan that death was considered most worthy in which the first attack upon life was made upon the seat of the properly psychic faculties; therefore the victim of *hara-kiri* rips open his belly and is then beheaded by his best friend so as to shorten the pain of death. It is, however, quite probable that Lao-tze in this connection really means what he literally says, viz., that the holy man, when he governs, empties the people's hearts of desires, but takes care of their bodily wants, i. e., "fills their stomachs and strengthens their bones."

The word *kuh* might be translated (as

[2] רַחֲמִים

in former editions) "backbone," but in the original it reads "bones." To make a man strong-boned means to render him steady in character. I prefer to translate the passage literally in all its roughness and will leave the interpretation of it to the reader.

CHAPTER 4.

The word *tsung*,[3] "arch-father," translates a Chinese term which means "patriarch, or first ancestor, founder of the family," and is frequently used with reference to Shang Ti, the Lord on High, in the sense of God.

The word *ch'an,* "dust," is a Buddhist term which means the worry of worldliness, and it is possible that this usage antedates Buddhism and that the word was current in the same sense in the time of Lao-tze. If that be so, if *ch'an* means the troubles of life, the travailing of the world, we offer the following alternate translation of the verse in which the word occurs:

[3] 宗

"It will blunt its own sharpness,
Will its tangles unravel;
It will dim its own radiance
And conform to its travail."

The same holds good in Chapter 56, where the same verse is quoted

CHAPTER 5.

In former editions the translator accepted the following version: "Heaven and earth exhibit no benevolence; to them the ten thousand things are like straw dogs. The holy man exhibits no benevolence; to him the hundred families are like straw dogs."

Does that mean that heaven and earth have a mode of procedure of their own; that their actions can not be measured by the usual standard of human benevolence? May we assume that human lives serve their purpose best if they become sacrifices just as strawdogs are offered on the altars of heaven and earth? This solution can neither be proved nor refuted, but it seems too modern.

We learn from the commentators that

straw dogs are burned in place of living dogs as sacrifices to heaven and earth, and so the reference to them means treatment without regard or consideration. It is possible that Lao-tze meant to say that "heaven and earth" treats all people with an impartial indifference as God makes his sun rise on the evil and on the good (compare Chapter 79). But Lao-tze might as well have meant the very opposite, that "if heaven and earth and also the sage were without benevolence, they would treat the people like straw dogs." The Chinese text seems to favor the former interpretation, but the first sentence may be conditional and then the latter rendering which has been adopted by Harlez would be correct.

The question is whether Lao-tze did or did not believe that heaven and earth and the Tao were endowed with sentiment. An answer will be difficult if not impossible, but I am now inclined to think that he was more of mystic than a philosopher, and he recognized in the dispensation of the world a paternal and loving providence.

The phrase "heaven and earth" has a deeper meaning to the Chinese than to us. According to Chinese notions the primordial essence, called *t'ai chi*,[4] "the great Ultimate," divided itself into two principles called Yin and Yang (mentioned in Chapter 42). The former is negative, female, dark, passive; the latter is positive, male, light and active. The former is represented by earth, the latter by heaven; the former by the moon, the latter by the sun. The "ten thousand things" (i. e., all existences in the world), owe their characters to different mixtures of these two elementary principles.

Emptiness is one of the virtues praised by Lao-tze, and the emptiness of heaven is to him an example of the emptiness which man ought to possess. By emptiness Lao-tze understands the absence of personal ambition, of desire, or to use

[4] In Chapter 28, 2, Lao-tze calls this same ultimate, *wu chi,* "the infinite." For further details see *Chinese Philosophy,* pages 24-34. Compare also page 167 in this book.

his own phrase, it is "the doing of the not-doing" (*wei wu wei*).

Lao-tze concludes the chapter with a homely saying concerning gossip, which acquires a deep and peculiar meaning in the context by comparing "fulsome talk" to the emptiness of heaven.

The Chinese text reads *to yen*, literally, "many words," i. e., gossip.

CHAPTER 6.

The verse quoted in this chapter seems to be the inscription over a fountain which it was claimed never ran dry. People believed that its source was deep and sprang from the root of heaven and earth, which would explain that its supply was inexhaustible. In using this quotation Lao-tze looks upon the spring as an emblem of the mysterious nature of the Tao.

The Manchu version translates the word *ku*, valley, as a verb by "nourishing," which makes a very good sense for the first line, thus:

"Who nourishes spirituality does not die."

The use of *ku* (valley) as a verb, meaning "to feed, to nourish, to quicken," according to all dictionaries, is quite common in Chinese. But we might as well interpret *ku* as an adjective or participle and translate (with Couvreur):[5]

"L'esprit vivifiant ne meurt pas."

A literal translation would read thus:

"The quickening spirit never dies.
It is called the mysterious woman.
The mysterious woman's gate
Is called of heaven and earth the root.
For ever and aye it abides
[And] its use is without effort."

The Manchu translator finds a physiological meaning in this chapter. Dr. Berthold Laufer has kindly furnished me with a translation of it as follows:
"Who nourishes the soul will not die. This is called the life of the main artery (*Kuhen-i ergen* = Chinese *yüen p'in*, "mysterious woman"). The door of the life of the main artery is called the root

[5] See his French-Chinese Dictionary, p. 447.

of procreation and increase. As if preserved for all eternity, it is inexhaustible in its practical application."[6]

Dr. Laufer adds: "It is strange that the Chinese words for 'heaven and earth' which otherwise are literally translated, are here rendered by the verbal nouns *banjibure* and *fusembure,* the former 'creating,' the latter 'increasing.'"

CHAPTER 9.

A German proverb says: "*Allzu scharf macht schartig.*" This is a truth which few learn, and so it is daily verified again and again in business, in politics and in private life.

The word *rh* is a copula often translated "and" or "but." The character depicts the side portions of the face, the whiskers, or the bristles of an animal, thus denoting something added or an extension. The sense of the chapter depends on the grammatical significance of this word, and we can scarcely be mistaken when we translate "Grasp to

[6] Literally: "Lasting preserved like; used if, inexhaustible."

the full, is it not likely stopped? Scheme to being sharp, will you be able long to guard [your position]?" The verb *jui* = scheme, means "to scrutinize, to examine," and *pao* = "to guard, to maintain, to protect, to defend."

CHAPTER 10.

The text of the first two sentences is difficult, and we deem our present version an improvement.[7] Literally the beginning seems to read thus: "Being insistent in disciplining the sense soul." Mr. Ng Poon Chew writes: "The first two characters are verbs, there is no question as to that. The word *poh* is commonly understood by the Chinese to be the passive half of the human soul equivalent to *yin* in nature."

The Manchu version (as Dr. Laufer informs me) in agreement with a Chinese quotation of this passage by Huai Nan Tze takes all these sentences as queries.

[7] For an explanation of the text see "Emendations and Comments," pp. ix-x in the second issue of *Lao-Tze's Tao-Teh-King.*

CHAPTER 11.

Things are shaped by carving, by taking away, by diminishing the material. Accordingly that which is no longer there, the non-existent, constitutes their worth. Thus it appears that the part in this case would be greater than the whole, or to state the same truth briefly "less is more." As Hesiod says in his Works and Days (30):

Νήπιοι οὐδ᾽ ἴσασιν ὅσῳ πλέον ἥμισυ παντός.

"Foolish they are, for they know not
That half than the whole is much greater."

CHAPTER 12.

The meaning of the verses quoted in this chapter carries out the principle enunciated in Chapter 11. The utility of things, as well as the worth of life, is attained not by having everything in completion and in fulness, but by selecting some parts and omitting others, by moderation and by discrete elimination. All the colors blind you, a discrete selection will make a picture. All the notes make a noise, while a few of them in proper succession make a melody. All the tastes mixed together are offensive, but a choice of them is pleasant.

Such is Lao-tze's method of teaching that the form of things is more important than substance. (See also Chapter 11.)

In former editions we have translated the quotation thus:

> "The five colors the human eye will blind,
> The five notes the human ear will rend,
> The five tastes the human mouth offend."

> "Racing and hunting will human hearts turn mad,
> Objects of prize make human conduct bad."

*   *   *

The phrase "he attends to the inner and not to the outer" reads in a literal translation "acts the stomach, not acts the eye."

The outer and the inner are called in Chapter 38 the flower and the fruit, the

former being the mere show, the latter
the true import of life.

CHAPTER 13.

The ruler or prime minister who attends to the government as he attends to
his own body, understanding that it is
a source of "great heartache," is worthy
of the trust.

The comparison of "rank" or "high
office" to the body as a source of great
trouble and anxiety is based on an idea
which also plays an important part in
Buddhism. Buddhist philosophy explains
that the cause of all earthly trouble is
due to the body, and the body ought to
be treated like a wound which is the
source of pain. We attend to it without
loving it. In the "Questions of King
Milinda" (*Milindapañha*) the Buddhist
saint Nagasena says: "They who have
retired from the world take care of their
bodies as though they were wounds without thereby becoming attached to them"
(Warren, *Buddhism in Translations,* p.
423). So long as man lives in his bodily
existence he is subject to anxiety; as

soon as he ceases to live in the flesh he is no more troubled.

The character *ching*, here translated "trembling," denotes the state of a shy horse, and the word "heartache" shows a heart with a cord above it, such as is used in China for stringing up coins.

The last sentence of this chapter has been omitted because, with the exception of one word, it is a literal repetition of the preceding sentence and seems to have slipped into the text by a copyist's mistake.

CHAPTER 14.

This chapter is remarkable for several reasons. Lao-tze speaks of the Tao and describes it by saying what it is not. It is not perceptible to the senses; accordingly it is "colorless," "soundless" and "bodiless." It cannot be seen, it cannot be heard, it cannot be touched; but this supersensible something, the purely relational in all things, the divine Reason, is one and the same throughout. It is the Unnamable, the cosmic law, the world-order which moulds all things.

Both its beginning and its end are wrapped in obscurity.

Lao-tze's expression, "the form of the formless," corresponds pretty closely to Kant's term "pure form"; it means the form which possesses no bodily shape, and as such it is equivalent to the Buddist term *arupo*.

It is strange that Lao-tze's description of the Tao finds an almost literal parallel in the Phædrus where Plato speaks of the presence of a being in the over-heaven, i. e., in the supercelestial place, a being not perceptible to the senses and to be apprehended only by the mind, the "pilot of the soul." This presence is described as an essence, truly existent,[8] without color, without shape and impalpable. Plato says:

Τὸν δὲ ὑπερουράνιον τόπον οὔτε τις ὕμνησέ πω τῶν τῇδε ποιητὴς οὔτε ποθ᾽ ὑμνήσει κατ᾽ ἀξίαν. ἔχει δὲ ὧδε. τολμητέον γὰρ οὖν τό γε ἀληθὲς εἰπεῖν ἄλλως τε καὶ περὶ ἀληθείας λέγοντα· ἡ γὰρ ἀχρωματός τε καὶ ἀσχημάτιστος καὶ ἀναφὴς οὐσία ὄντως ψυχῆς οὖσα κυβερνήτῃ μόνῳ θεατὴ νῷ· περὶ ἣν τὸ τῆς ἀληθοῦς ἐπιστήμης γένος τοῦτον ἔχει τὸν τόπον.

[8] ὄντως ὄν.

In Jowett's translation this reads:

"Of the heaven which is above the heavens, what earthly poet ever did or ever will sing worthily? It is such as I shall describe; for I must dare to speak the truth, when truth is my theme. There abides the very being with which true knowledge is concerned; the colorless, the formless, the intangible essence visible only to mind, who is the pilot of the soul."—Phaedrus, pag. 247.

The Latin version of the most important part of the passage reads thus:

"Nam essentia vere existens, sine colore, sine figura, sine tactu."

The similarity with Lao-tze is obvious, only the second term, in Chinese "soundless," or "inaudible," is omitted, while the Greek "shapeless," viz., non-material or having no body, has absolutely the same meaning as the Chinese.

* * *

In addition to this surprising similarity between Lao-tze's very words and the thoughts of a philosopher who lived about 200 years after him in ancient

Greece, a distant country which at that time was in no connection with China, we must point out another strange coincidence. The three words, "colorless," "soundless" and "incorporeal," read in Chinese *i, ki, wei,* and the French scholar Abel Rémusat saw in this combination of Chinese characters the corresponding three Hebrew letters, *Jod, Heh, Vav,* indicating the name Jehovah, and his theory was accepted by many others who for some reason or other believed that there ought to have been a mysterious prehistoric connection between the Chinese and the Israelites. The theory has found the support of a German translator of Lao-tze's book, Victor von Strauss, a confessed mystic, but it is not countenanced by any other sinologist of standing, and there is no need to refute it. We see in it a curious though quite remarkable coincidence.

* * *

Liquids generally are clear at the top and sediments settle at the bottom, but here Lao-tze, using the simile, reverses the statement by saying that in its upper portion the Tao is not clear and in its lower strata it is not obscure. If we had not to deal with an author like Lao-tze who loves to mystify we might assume some mistake in the text, but as the statement stands it reminds us of St. Augustine's description of Christianity when he compares religious truth to an immeasurable ocean in whose waters a lamb may wade, while an elephant must swim. The simple mind of a child finds no difficulty in understanding the meaning of the Tao while a scholar may not be able to fathom its depth. We may also say that the deeper problems of philosophy are in their general aspect quite simple, but the superficial applications obscure them by complexity.

CHAPTER 15.

Lao-tze frequently quotes proverbs of the people and sayings of his predecessors. Of the latter he has a very high opinion which he here expresses.

Lao-tze says that the sages of yore behave like guests, alluding to the Chi-

nese custom for guests to be always reserved and modest. They are elusive
as the Tao is elusive (see Chapter 21),
which means that their words admit of
more than one interpretation and frequently conceal a deeper meaning. In
the same sense the Tao is called elusive
because it has never been grasped in its
full significance. A philosopher may
think he has fathomed its meaning, and
afterwards may find out that his view is
only one aspect and there is more to it.
So a search for truth can never be completed. Like melting ice the old masters
have more depth than the surface shows.

Further, the sages are simple, without
the polish of artful elegance, and thus
they are compared to "rough wood."
They are empty because they make no
show, and they are like the valley, which
is Lao-tze's favorite simile to indicate
an attitude of lowliness. The more lowly
a river flows the larger and broader will
it be, and the most lowly valley will become the main stream, the ocean river,
of an entire system with many tribu-
taries.

The last sentence of this chapter is difficult to interpret, and had perhaps better be translated:

"Without being fashionable he is perfect,"

which would mean "though not in style he is as he ought to be." The last three words read in literal translation "not-new-perfected" which may mean "not newly formed," that is to say, "he is not of a modern fashion"; or we may translate, "he is not fashionable and yet perfect"; or "without being renewed he is complete," which would imply that the sage can grow old without standing in need of rejuvenescence, viz., natural or artificial means of recuperating his vitality. But it may mean, as we have translated it in a former edition, "without reform he is perfect." Finally the two last words may be synonyms, and the three may mean, "without being renewed and completed."

Happily the passage is not of much consequence, and there is no great harm if we can not decide which interpretation is preferable.

CHAPTER 18.

This chapter is directed against the Confucianist morality of filial piety, loyalty, and justice. Lao-tze is disgusted with the very words. Where the Tao obtains there is no need of preaching justice, filial piety and loyalty, for the vitrue of the Tao is spontaneous. The men whose hearts are bare of these virtues, parade them in words.

CHAPTER 19.

The display which obtains in Confucian ethics is here condemned, and Lao-tze's words remind us of Christ's warnings against the self-righteousness of the Pharisees. Lao-tze wants us to abandon: (1) saintliness and prudence, (2) benevolence and justice, (3) smartness and greed. He declares that culture (i. e., Confucian morality) is insufficient to accomplish these three things. He advises:

"Hold fast that which endures,
Mind simplicity, preserve purity,
Lessen self, diminish desire."

The word "learnedness" in contrast to wisdom means the artificial scholarship of Confucian literati, who like the Pharisees of the New Testament insist on external propriety more than on a regeneration of the heart.

CHAPTER 20.

Lao-tze continues to criticize Confucianism as represented by the learned ones, the literati. According to Confucius conventional propriety is a great virtue, and it is very important that people reply according to the properly established modes of speaking. There are two forms of affirmation in Chinese: One is pronounced *wei,* and being straightforward and manly it is proper for men and boys to use; the other, pronounced *o,* is modest, and it behooves women and girls to employ no other form of expressing assent. Lao-tze would not insist on the significance of such externalities, and so he says, "What is the difference between 'yea' and 'yes'? There is none. But there is a difference between bad and good."

In times of disorder lives are constantly endangered and the people become indifferent to death. This is not the natural state of things and ought to be avoided. Lao-tze's warning is illustrated in modern history by the French Revolution when the prisoners of the terrorist government actually joked about the guillotine and went to the place of execution with absolute unconcern. Similar conditions prevailed in China in the days of Lao-tze.

In this chapter, as well as further down (Chapters 72 and 74), the old philosopher makes reference to the prevalence of great disturbances which make the people restless. A Chinese Jeremiah, forlorn among people who only thought of enjoying themselves, he burst out into bitter lamentation, and we cannot read these lines without feeling compassion for the sage who differed so much from the rest of the world.

The fourth and eighth sections of this chapter recall Christ's saying (Matt. viii. 20): "The foxes have holes, and the

birds of the air have nests; but the Son
of man hath not where to lay his head."

CHAPTER 21.

The last two lines of the quoted verse
in Chapter 21 are obscure in the original Chinese. The difficulty lies in the
meaning of the word *fu,* which means
anything that is first, either in time or
dignity. Literally the eight words read:
"Its—name—not—departs; Thereby—
it notes—all—the first."

The sense seems to be that the Tao is
eternal, for its name never departs.
Therefore it has been in the beginning
of creation. In this sense we have translated the passage in former editions:

"Its name does not depart
Thence lo! All things take start."

which means, "It is of all the first."

Should *fu,* however, have to be taken
in the sense of excellence we would propose either of these two readings:

"Its name does not pass hence
Lo! Here's all excellence!"

or, if we lay stress on the verb *yüeh,* "it beholds," we translate:

"Its name is never vanishing
It heeds the good in everything."

Mr. Ng Poon Chew favors the idea that the character *fu* means "the beginning."

The Manchu version follows the last interpretation. Dr. Laufer translates: "Hence one investigates all good things," —which seems to mean: "Thereby we learn what in all things is good," and the concluding sentence would read: "Whereby do I know what is good in all things? Through IT." In other words: Reason is the standard of excellence."

The two last words "through IT" in this chapter comprise a favorite term of Lao-tze, and by "IT" Lao-tze means "Reason."

CHAPTER 22.

Lao-tze here as in many other places quotes a sentiment from the sages of yore.

These beautiful lines remind us of several Biblical sayings, such as "The crooked shall be made straight" (Is. xl. 4) and "The bruised reed shall he not break" (Matt. xii. 20). Compare also the beatitude that those who mourn shall be comforted (Matt. v. 4).

It is strange, however, that though Christ's Gospel agrees in spirit so well with Lao-tze's philosophy he states the very opposite to the sentiment of the last two lines, saying: "For whosoever hath, to him shall be given, and he shall have more abundance: but whosoever hath not, from him shall be taken away even that he hath" (Matt. xiii. 12).

The Chinese words *ch'ü* and *ch'üen* here translated "crooked" and "crushed" may be taken in the physical sense as "the distorted ones" and also figuratively, denoting those morally awry or wrong-doers.

The character *hwo* shows "a heart" and "doubt," the latter being the phonetic (*hwo*). It means "to delude, to blind, to embarrass, to bewilder, to un-

settle," and we have translated it by
"grieve."

The last two lines of the quotation
might also be interpreted to mean,
"What is too little shall receive more;
what is too much shall be in a state of
perplexity." See also Chapter 77, 1-3.

Compare the second section of this
chapter with Chapter 24.

CHAPTER 24.

Mr. Medhurst translates the first sentence: "Who tiptoes totters; who strad-
dles stumbles."

The translator trusts that the style of
this chapter has been greatly improved
in this edition. The first section has
been made more terse, and in the second
the sense comes out more clearly. *Yü
shih,* in former editions translated "of-
fal of food," means "too much of food"
and is better interpreted as a surfeit of
food. Further we have in former editions translated *chui hing* as "excrescence in the system." The word *chui* (a
synonym of *yü*) denotes anything that
is redundant, an excrescence, or a wen,

and *hing* is a peculiar word which literally means "to go," or "to walk," and may mean the way of acting, or the bodily system, or almost anything else. We might translate *chui hing* "overdoing in behavior," but it is likely that Lao-tze actually meant that the overdoing of self-display is like a wen in the face— too much and therefore disgusting. Laotze may also think of Confucian supererogatory behavior, which is characterized by overdoing in politeness and is offensive to the man who believes in the simple life.

The new interpretation is supported by the Manchu version.

The lines here quoted are parallel to the lines in the second section of Chapter 23. The same words are used, only the negation *pu* is differently placed so as to produce a contrast.

CHAPTER 25.

The word *shi,* "departing," may very well be understood in the sense of dying.

The word *fan* means literally "return," denoting "coming back," and in order to imitate the terse Chinese text, the best translation for "having come back" is "home." Lao-tze says: "Reason, the great distant beyond, is our home."

Section 5 seems to be a gloss which slipped into the text. At any rate the bracketed portion is too trivial to come from the hand of Lao-tze.

CHAPTER 26.

The word *tsz'*, translated "gravity," is a peculiar phrase which literally means "baggage wagon." The intermediate idea seems to be "heaviness" or "gravity," the latter in the double sense (literal and figurative) as used in English.

In our former edition it was translated "dignity."

CHAPTER 27.

In Section 4 we have adopted an entirely new interpretation. In following a suggestion of Prof. H. A. Giles, we construe the two characters *shan* (words 6 and 14) denoting "good" or "goodness," as verbs in the sense to consider as good, and translate "to respect"; and further the characters *shi* (words 9 and 21) in their common meaning as "multitudes," not as we had it in former editions (though it is not wrong), as "educator."

CHAPTER 28.

In order to understand what Lao-tze means by manhood and womanhood, by brightness and blackness, by fame and shame, we must bear in mind what has been said above in the explanation of Chapter 5 about the two principles Yin and Yang. Compare also Lao-tze's views about honoring the right in times of war and the left in times of peace (Chapter 31). Manliness is not worth much unless tempered by womanliness, and a good warrior is not warlike, a good fighter is not pugnacious (Chap. 68).

The word *chih* means "to carve, to form, to regulate," and as a noun "law" or "norm." Lao-tze seems to mean that a government which upholds great principles and rules according to the maxims of the Tao can never do any harm.

Professor Giles translates, "a great principle can not be divided," which

he interprets to mean, that it applies
universally. (See Emendations and
Comments to *Lao-Tze's Tao-Teh-King*,
pp. xxi-xxii.)

CHAPTER 29.

The doctrine of "doing the not-doing"
has rightly been compared to the French
principle of *laissez faire*, although the
two are not the same. Lao-tze wants
to say here that "he who makes, mars";
we therefore should not interfere but
let everything take the course of its
natural development.

CHAPTER 35.

The world is noisy. There is music;
there are dainties to eat; there are many
distractions, and the passing stranger
stops. The Tao is tasteless, is invisible,
is inaudible, but inexhaustible in its use.
We have here a trinity of the negative
qualities of the Tao just as in Chapter
14. Compare also Chapter 42.

CHAPTER 36.

The tendency of the world is to acquire hardness and strength, but in this

chapter the sage warns us to beware of
these qualities, and rather remain tender
and weak. The people should scarcely
know that weapons exist.

On the authority of Professor Giles
the last section of this chapter should
read "Fishes can not be taken away from
the water. The instruments of government can not be delegated to others."
Huai Nan Tze tells a story of a sover-
eign who lost his throne by transferring
the power of punishment to his minister.
(See Emendations and Comments to *Lao-
Tze's Tao-Teh-King,* second issue, pages
xvi-xvii.)

Lao-tze regarded acquaintance with
weapons as an unnatural condition which
would prove fatal to the people, just as
fish must die when they are removed
from their natural element, the water.

CHAPTER 38.

Justice is different from virtue and
benevolence. It is the nature of justice
to act and enforce its pretensions.

True or superior virtue is here called
"unvirtue" because it does not make a

show of virtue; it does not "act virtue."
A difference between virtue and justice
is that justice doling out punishments
must make a show of its power, and so
"acts and makes pretensions." It is obvious that here the Confucian conception of virtue is criticised for the reason that it is always in evidence and is
therefore inferior,—it is shoddy.

Traditionalism (*ts'ien shih*, "of times
bygone the knowledge") which is mentioned further on in this chapter is a
characteristic feature of Confucian ethics.

In former editions I took *ts'ien* in the
sense of "early" or "premature" and
translated "quickwittedness"; but we
must bear in mind that we have before
us a criticism of Confucian ethics with
its rules of propriety based upon a reverence for the past, clinging tenaciously
to tradition. Lao-tze says that this respect for bygone times, this traditionalism is not commendable. It is but "the
flower of reason," meaning thereby that
it makes a display or show of virtue;

it parades morality but it does not contain the fruit.

CHAPTER 39.

Plato scholars will note that the famous dialogue "Parmenides," discussing the problem of the one and the many, may fitly be compared with Lao-tze's exposition of the nature of oneness, the poetical portion of which sounds like a philosophical rhapsody.

The simile that the carriage does not consist of its parts, but it a definite combination of its parts, is also used in the Buddhist book, "Questions of King Milinda," written several centuries after Lao-tze.

* * *

The last line in section 7, *Ta fang wu yü* (literally, "Greatest square has no corner") should be compared with the same sentiment in Chapter 45, *ta chih joh ch'ü* ("greatest straightness seems curved").

CHAPTER 42.

The subject of oneness or unity treated in Chapter 39 is here continued, and

unity is represented as the product of
the Tao or Reason.

The trinity idea plays an important
part in human thought almost everywhere, in philosophical systems and in
many religions including Christianity.
The Chinese idea of trinity is based
on the notion that there are two opposed
principles, Yang and Yin, which have
originated, as Lao-tze explains, from a
primordial oneness, called by Cheu-tze
and other later philosophers *Chi,* the
ultimate, or the absolute. Oneness produces by differentiation a twohood, viz.,
the twohood of Yang, or heaven, and
Yin, or earth. Between heaven and earth
is the air, *Ch'i,* the breath of life; and
from this trinity of Yang, Yin and Ch'i
all things are derived.

Incidentally we must warn the reader
that *chi,* the ultimate,[1] is quite different from *ch'i,* breath.[2]

[1] 極 *Chi* is used by Lao-tze in its ordinary
sense in Chapter 16, and 68, last word. For
the philosophical terms *t'ai chi* and *wu chi*
see p. 138 and compare Giles's Dictionary,
No. 859.

[2] 氣 *Ch'i,* breath, occurs three times in our

The words *ku kwa*, here translated "orphaned, lonely," mean, the former "a fatherless son," and the latter "lonely"; and in this sense the emperor has been called the "lonely one" as one who stands aloof, who is solitary, peerless and without equal. But the original meaning is still prominent in the term and so we may look upon Lao-tze's use of the word as a pun which he uses as a peg upon which to hang a lesson. The word *kwa,* "lonely," has the meaning of "little" and "insignificant" which in agreement with a Chinese view of politeness is also used in the sense of "your humble servant," or as the Germans say, *meine Wenigkeit,* which may justly be considered an adequate equivalent for the Chinese *kwa.*

The term *pu ku* is used in the same sense as *kwa,* meaning literally "not worthy," as a modest expression in which the speaker refers to himself. It serves so commonly as an equivalent for the

text: (1) translated "airs" in Sze ma Tsien's biography of Lao-tze; (2) translated "vitality" in Chapter 10; and (3) "breath," in Chapter 42. See Giles's Dictionary No. 1064. The word is also transcribed *k'i.*

pronoun of the first person that even
the emperor does not scorn it. However
the former words *ku kwa* denote the emperor as a peerless person, the only one
of his kind, the man who has no equal.

* * *

Lao-tze is certainly an original thinker
and yet he disclaims originality; he constantly quotes his predecessors, but he
reads his own thoughts into their sayings. He says here, "What others have
taught I teach also," but in Chapter 15
he says that they are too profound to
be understood, and so he endeavors to
make them intelligible.

* * *

The chapter concludes with a statement which tradition explains as meaning that he will "expound the doctrine's
foundation," but the literal reading of
the last six words runs thus:
"I shall do the doctrine's father."
The word *fu,* "father," pictures a hand
with a rod and means "rule, authority,
father, fatherly or loving." It is the
most common word for "father" and

ought to be so translated unless weighty reasons speak against it.

The word *wei,* commonly translated "to do," may mean "to live up to, to actualize, to exemplify, to do the will of, to obey." Obviously it means the actual doing, not the purely theoretical expounding, and so we explain the passage to mean, "While the mass of mankind are violent and self-willed, which leads to trouble and an unnatural death, I mean to exemplify in my life the will of the doctrine's father," or in a more literal rendering "But I will obey the doctrine's father (i. e., the Tao)."

CHAPTER 45.

Literally the second quotation reads:
"Greatest straightness is like a curve,
Greatest skill is like awkwardness,
Greatest eloquence is like stammering."

The first line reminds us of modern geometry where the straight line may be regarded as a curve of an infinitely small curvature. Cf. note on Chapter 41.

CHAPTER 47.

Whether or not Lao-tze meant it, he here endorses Kant's doctrine of the *a priori,* which means that certain truths can be stated *a priori,* viz., even before we make an actual experience. It is not the globe trotter who knows mankind, but the thinker. In order to know the sun's chemical composition we need not go to the sun; we can analyze the sun's light by spectrum analysis. We need not stretch a tape line to the moon to measure its distance from the earth, we can calculate it by the methods of an *a priori* science (trigonometry).

CHAPTER 49.

The word *shang* means "constant, ordinary, usual, common" etc., and the contrast requires the sense that the saint has not the heart as other people have, which means a heart of his own.

The "one hundred families" is a Chinese term which means the people of a district.

The second section of this chapter contains a difficulty in the text. Its third sentence reads in the Chinese text as translated in our former editions, "Virtue is good"; but this does not make good sense, as it is trivial. While pondering over the meaning of these two characters the translator discovered two versions[9] which replace the word *teh,* "virtue," by its homophone, *teh,* "to obtain," and it seemed quite probable that this was the original reading. The change from *teh,* "to obtain," to *teh,* "virtue," could naturally and at an early date have originated through a careless scribe in a book where the word *teh,* "virtue," occurred so frequently. Once introduced, the mistake could easily have been perpetuated in the text.

The word *teh,* "to obtain," makes good sense and might even suggest itself as the most appropriate text emendation. On the ground of this consideration we might prefer the reading *teh,* "to ob-

[9] See the Emendations and Comments to the second issue of the author's *Lao-Tze's Tao-Teh-King,* p. vii.

tain," and propose to translate the passage thus:

"The good I meet with goodness, the bad I also meet with goodness; thus I obtain goodness (i. e., I actualize virtue.) The faithful I meet with faith, the faithless I also meet with faith; thus I obtain faith (i. e., I actualize faith)."

In other words, we must meet not only the good with goodness but the bad also with goodness, if we want to actualize the ideal of goodness; and we must meet not only the faithful with faith but the faithless also with faith, in order to actualize the ideal of faith.

This is the obvious meaning of Laotze, for he here expresses his view of the way a man can become truly good and faithful. He does not admit any utilitarian argument and lays down the rule for a man who follows the Tao. He can be truly good and truly faithful only if he is good and faithful to all, whether he has to deal with the good or the not-good, the faithful or the faithless.

The Manchu translator had before him a text which read *teh,* "virtue," not *teh,* "obtain," but he construes *teh*, "virtue," as a genitive. If he is right, we must translate, "That is virtue's goodness," and further down, "That is virtue's faith."

After some hesitation we have finally adopted the interpretation of the Manchu version.

CHAPTER 50.

The first line of this chapter contains much food for thought. In our first edition we have translated these four words by "Going forth is life, coming home is death." We still cling to the same meaning, but we believe we have improved the diction by translating "Abroad in life, home in death."

We must grant, however, that we might translate, "He who enters life must return in death," but this interpretation that "he who is born must die," is objectionable mainly because it is too trivial for Lao-tze

The second paragraph in this chapter is obscure and seems beyond hope of

making good sense. A literal translation reads:

"Life's followers [are] ten have three
Death's followers [are] ten have three
In man's life the moving to death
places are also ten have three."

This may mean either ten plus three,
i. e., thirteen, or of ten take three, viz.,
"three in ten."

If the translation "thirteen" be correct, "thirteen retainers" might according to Chinese folklore mean the five
senses and the eight apertures which
make thirteen avenues of life. This
interpretation is based on the view of
the commentator Lu Tze who may be
right, and his view becomes somewhat
probable when we bear in mind Chapter
52, where Lao-tze speaks of the mouth
and the sense-gates as beset with danger.
There he declares that the sage who
keeps these openings closed will to the
end of his life remain safe.

I applied to Mr. Ng Poon Chew for
an explanation and he writes:

"The passage is very vague and obscure, its meaning is no clearer to me

than to you. I have consulted a few good Chinese scholars and they were all baffled. The words *shi yiu san*, "ten have three," may mean here "thirteen" or "three out of ten."

If we translate "three in ten," the reader will naturally ask, Three times three in ten make nine, where is the tenth? And we would answer, it is "the man who bases his life on goodness." Three in ten are anxious to live, three in ten somehow are doomed to death, and other three in ten walk blindly toward death; they all live life's intensity. There is but one who is above life and death, and this is the man who bases his life on goodness.

In this case we interpret the word *fu*, "footman, follower, retainer," in the sense of "pursuer."

We have chosen the former interpretation which seems to us the most probable, but do not claim to have solved the difficulty.

* * *

The last section of this chapter finds a striking parallel in Plato's Phaedrus,

in the same book and on the same *pagina*
(248) that contains the reference to the
supercelestial being which is colorless
and shapeless, quoted above in our comments on Chapter 14. The passage in
Plato reads: "There is a law of destiny
that the soul which attains any vision
of truth in company with a god is preserved from harm until the next period,
and if attaining always is always un-
harmed."[10]

The same idea is expressed in the
famous ode of Horace, *Integer vitae.*
The belief that a truly good man is
miraculously protected in danger is not
uncommon in folktales and appears to
have been an integral part of primitive
religion.

Are these coincidences between Plato
and Lao-tze accidental or are we to look
upon them as echoes of a notion which in
both the West and East have been in-
herited from a distant prehistoric past?
The latter is certainly not improbable.

* * *

"Reality" here translates the word

[10] Jowett's translation.

wuh, "concrete things," and commonly
occurs in the phrase "the ten thousand
things" which means the entire world.

The character *sh'* = "expansion" is a
synonym of *wei* in the sense of assertion. The sage fears to be or to appear
or to claim too much. He avoids self-
aggrandizement.

CHAPTER 54.

This chapter, like so many other passages, is directed against the Confu-
cianists who in their ethics insist on
the ritual of ancestral sacrifices. Lao-
tze believes that wherever the Tao is ob-
served, filial piety and sacrificial celebrations will be spontaneous.

CHAPTER 56.

The quotation is the same as in Chapter 4, only here it is attributed to the
sage, in the former place to the Tao.
The sage identifies himself with the mor-
tal coil he is heir to, with *ch'an,* his dust
or the troubles of his bodily life, and this
is called here "a profound identification." Even in the lowliness of his con-

dition the sage feels his own dignity as a man of the Tao.

This same idea has produced the conception of the god-man in Christianity as well as in pagan religions.

CHAPTER 57.

When, as Hamlet says, "the time is out of joint," we observe that political disorder produces restlessness among the people and in its wake come startling events. The people are frightened and superstition dominates their minds. The result is that ghosts will spook and the gods will be angry, as stated in Chapter 60.

CHAPTER 59.

The "mother of the commonwealth" is commonly interpreted to be thrift. It is not impossible that Lao-tze means the Tao or Reason, but in the same chapter he uses the term Tao in the more general sense as "way."

CHAPTER 60.

Whatever the first sentence of this chapter may mean, it is oddly expressed.

One should govern a country as one would fry small fish, and we have added the traditional explanation in brackets, "neither gut nor scale them," which means the same as the rule *wei wu wei*, i. e., do the not-doing, practice non-practice; leave them alone and do not meddle with their affairs.

In ancient times ghosts were feared, and ghosts begin to spook, or at least are believed to spook, where crimes keep the minds of the people in a state of fearful and unsettled expectancy. See Chapter 57.

CHAPTER 61.

This chapter contains more wisdom than it seems to possess at first sight. The same idea is expressed in the English saying that by stooping one conquers. It is also echoed in the New Testament where Jesus says that he who wishes to be the master of all should be their servant. In an empire or confederacy of states that state takes the lead which renders the greatest service to the others. For instance Prussia took the lead in Germany because through its systematic administration and well-organized army it offered protection and other advantages to the smaller states and so served their interests. In the same way Athens gained and lost ascendency in Greece; its downfall dates from the time when it ceased to serve the others and began to misuse its power. Since the loss of the thirteen American colonies England has adopted the same maxim of serving the interests of her dependencies. This policy which has proved successful and has repeatedly saved the British empire from dismemberment, was pronounced by Lao-tze in plain terms two and a half millenniums ago.

CHAPTER 62.

The proposition that "when sought the Tao is obtained," reminds one of the New Testament verse, "Seek and ye shall find."

CHAPTER 63.

In the famous passage, "Requite hatred with virtue," the word *teh*, "virtue," is

commonly translated "goodness." **We**
grant that this is the meaning, but we
prefer a literal rendering. The sentence
recalls Christ's injunction, "Love your
enemies," but it means that we should
treat those who hate us with justice and
goodness, according to the rules of the
Tao, the eternal Reason. It is not so
emphatic as the Christian saying, but it
is more logical and less paradoxical.

The sentence before the last means:
Rash promises are easily made; and if
we take things easy in the beginning
without thinking of the consequences we
shall soon be involved in complications.

CHAPTER 64.

The last word here translated by "interfere" is in Chinese *wei,* "to do" or
"to act."

The terms "likely" and "unlikely" are
literal translations of the Chinese.
Likely apparently means what is common or usual, and the unlikely, what is
unusual.

CHAPTER 70.

When Lao-tze says, "words have an ancestor, deeds have a master," he personifies Reason which makes the conception of Tao resemble Christian theism; but we can not deny that in this atmosphere of abstract thought the expressions, "ancestor" and "master" may be regarded as intentional similes, just as in other chapters the Tao is compared to a "father" (Chapters 4 and 42), a "mother" (Chapter 20, also 1 and 52), "the Lord" (Chapter 4) and the "great carpenter" (Chapter 74). Nevertheless the fact remains that Lao-tze has repeatedly personified the Tao in spite of its abstract nature.

CHAPTER 71.

The passage "to know the unknowable" is a smooth and quite correct translation, but there is a deeper sense in it and it certainly should not be interpreted in the sense of agnosticism. A strictly correct literal translation should read "know the not-knowing," which means "be familiar with that state of mind where knowing (the noetic faculty) is not the medium of our mental life." It is an expression of Lao-tze's mysticism in which the attitude of heart is considered superior to comprehension, and seems to involve what European mystics call intuition and what is characterized by St. Paul as the "peace that passeth understanding." We can retain the translation "unknowable" if it is understood in this sense, not as anything incomprehensible, an x in cognition, but as a mental attitude, as the feeling of the ineffable.

* * *

The connection between the first and second paragraphs consists in the idea that courage is sometimes successful and sometimes it brings harm. We do not know the reason why heaven sometimes dooms a hero. The word "doom," translated in the text "reject," reads in the Chinese "hate."

CHAPTER 74.

The "great carpenter who hews" is undoubtedly the Tao, or as theists would say, God. Compare our comment on Chapter 70.

We read in the Bible, "Vengeance is mine; I will repay, saith the Lord."

CHAPTER 75.

The last sentence finds its parallel in the New Testament (John xii. 25) where we read: "He that loveth his life shall lose it; and he that hateth his life in this world shall keep it unto life eternal."

CHAPTER 78,

In China the emperor takes the guilt of the whole nation upon himself when he brings his annual sacrifice, a full burnt offering, to Shang Ti the Lord on High, and this is expressed in the quotation of this chapter which thus bears a remarkable similarity to the Christian doctrine that Christ as the High Priest takes the sins of mankind upon his own shoulders. Here is another coincidence of the East with the West. The priest according to the primitive custom speaks in the name of the sacrificial animal, and the sacrificial animal represents the god himself.

CHAPTER 79.

The original reads, "The holy man keeps the left (*tso*) of contract" and *tso*, "left," means the debit side. The right side of the contract table contained the claims, *ch'eh,* which in its original meaning denotes "to go through" and then "that which can be enacted."

CHAPTER 80.

Lao-tze is not in favor of progress. He is bent on preaching that the Tao can be actualized in primitive conditions as well as, if not more easily than, in a highly complicated state of civilization. His ideal is not the luxury of wealth and power and learnedness, but the simple life of simple-minded people. He may even be accused of reactionary tendencies, for he is ready to abandon the

advance made by his predecessors up to
his own time and give up the practice
of writing on bamboo slips, in favor of
the prehistoric mode of keeping memo-
randa by knotted cords (*chieh shing*), or
as they are now called with an American
name, *quipu,* a method of assisting the
memory by threads of various dyes knotted in special ways.

Lao-tze will scarcely find followers for
his proposal to revert to primitive conditions, but even here where he is mistaken, there is a truth at the bottom
of his thought. It is the ideal of a simple life, so much preached and so little
practised in our days. Progress not only
brings new inventions but also loosens
the old ideals of simplicity, purity, hon-
esty and faith. In place of the restful
contentedness of former ages, the new
generation is filled with desires. People
have become reckless, arrogant, and lux-
urious. Learnedness takes the place of
wisdom, and a pretentious display of
filial piety supplants spontaneous respect for parents.

TABLE OF REFERENCES.

[The numbers refer to chapters of the text.]

Desires fewer, 19.
Desireless, Holy man desires to be, 64; Reason ever,
34; Who is found, 1.
Desolation, No end of, 20.
Differ from others, 20. Compare "Unlikely."
Difficult and easy, 63.
Diplomacy, No, 48, 53, 57.
Discipline of the senses, 10.
Discontent a misery, 46.
Disdain like a stone, 39.
Disorder, Beginning of, 38; When clans decay through,
18.
Display, Makes a, 2; Holy man does not, 72, 77.
Distant, Viewing the, 47.
Doom, Brings its own, 9.
Doors and windows, Cutting out, 11.
Dotage leads to squandering, 44.
Dread, death, People, 74; What people, 20.
Dreadful, The, 72.
Drinking, Excessive in, 53.
Duality, 42.
Duration, Forever lasteth his, 44.
Dust, One with its, 56.
Dwell not in the external, 38; on merit, Holy man
does not, 2, 77.

Ear, Five notes confound the, 12. See also "Outer."
Earth, is lasting, 7; is man's standard, 25.
Easy, and difficult, 2, 63; to understand, My words are,
70.
Economy, 67.
Eloquence stammers, 45.
Eluding, Reason's nature is, 21.
Elusive, Masters of yore, 15.
Empire, a divine vessel, 29; King of, 78; Model of, 28;
Not fit to take the, 48; Too light for the, 26; Trusted
with the, 13; Wife of the, 61.
Empties, Holy man, 3.

INDEX.

[The numbers refer to pages of this book. This is an Index to the Foreword, the Introduction and the Comments (pp. 3–22 and pp. 131–188). For passages in the *Canon of Reason and Virtue* the reader should look up the Table of References.]

Symbol of the T'ai Chi, the Great Ultimate.